lonely planet

D0881958

MICRO
NATIONS

John Ryan
George Dunford
Simon Sellars

Micronations: The Lonely Planet Guide to Home-Made Nations
September 2006

Published by
Lonely Planet Publications Pty Ltd
ABN 36 005 607 983

Lonely Planet Offices
Australia Locked Bag 1, Footscray, Victoria 3011
USA 150 Linden St, Oakland, CA 94607
UK 72-82 Rosebery Avenue, London EC1R 4RW

ISBN 1 74104 730 7

Contents

Introduction

> Membership in the UN is open to all peace-loving states which accept the obligations of the Charter and, in the judgement of the Organization, are willing and able to carry out these obligations.
>
> The admission of any such State to membership in the UN will be effected by a decision of the General Assembly upon the recommendation of the Security Council.
>
> *Article 4, Chapter 2, UN Charter*

> You can't be a real country unless you have a beer and an airline – it helps if you have some kind of a football team, or some nuclear weapons, but at the very least you need a beer.
>
> *Frank Zappa*

Everyone in the world shares a common bond. Our basic humanity connects everyone on this tiny planet in a fundamental way. But – being human – we prefer to focus on our differences. It's more fun.

Of all the things that make us different from – and sometimes puts us in conflict with – the people around us, our nationality is top of the tree. But nationality is also a great connector. When you're in a foreign place and you meet someone else from your place, an immediate and unspoken bond forms. It's a universal truth: you are always from somewhere.

Throughout history, some people have gone to great lengths to change where they're from. Obviously we can't change where we're born, but – whether through migration, naturalisation or just moving to the next town – we can change the place that we call home.

Micronations: The Lonely Planet Guide to Home-Made Nations is a journey across the world and into the minds of people who have decided to strike out against society, take control of their lives and change 'home'. But these people aren't satisfied with just moving to another town or country.

Their answer to the question 'Where are you from?' is revealing on many levels: they're from the Principality of Sealand, the Barony of Caux, Whangamomona and North Dumpling Island. These people – kings, archdukes, serene highnesses and presidents – are the creators of their own ethnic identity. They have become their hobby, and the results – as you will discover – are hilarious, inspiring and sometimes a little bit scary. But mostly hilarious.

What do we do with the childhood fantasy of being the boss of everything? This book is about those DIY pioneers who reject traditional methods of attaining power (elections, coups, owning a tobacco company, etc), and decide to create their own nations from scratch.

THE WHAT & THE WHERE

So what is a micronation? The people in this book have decided, for various reasons, to create their own nations. Some are theoretical experiments in statehood – examples of how nations should or could be organised. Others are played mostly for laughs – enormous, time-consuming, intricate jokes, usually made at the creator's own expense. Some of the more enduring nations are formed out of anger or discontent, frustration or desperation. Of these, there might even be a few sinister nations with unsound agendas…

This book is not concerned with the challenges faced by recognised nations that are small, such as Lichtenstein, Tuvalu or even San Marino. Sure, rising ocean levels, border disputes and ethnic identity are valid topics. But for our purposes, they're too valid.

Nor are we profiling nations with disputed – but indisputably real – claims for nation status. There's no Palestine in this book. No Somaliland, Azawad or Kingdom of Biffeche in Africa. No European Basque state or Trans-Dniestr Republic. Dhofar in Oman, the Principality of Mustang in Nepal, and Arakan in Myanmar don't make it either. And we're not touching Taiwan or West Papua with a bargepole.

While these places (and maybe a hundred more like them) all have rich and fascinating histories, and are well worth a look for people interested in the real world, they are not for us here.

We're also steering wide of the many hundreds of landless, virtual nations. Found mostly on the Internet and in the febrile imaginings of youngsters, these nations create governments, encourage citizenship, make and break treaties, carp, in-fight, throw tantrums and generally behave like the real UN. Phrases like 'virtual immanent global sovereignty' and 'sovereign nonterritorial nation' are used with regularity within this group. So while travellers can't actually visit these nations (probably just as well, given their tendency to use phrases such as these), we've given the best of them a brief mention near the end of the book (p128).

And, finally, we've decided to exclude some micronations on the grounds that they're a bit too serious or a bit…well… dubious. Events in Waco, Texas, in 1993 involving a separatist cult called the Branch Davidian demonstrated that there can be a tragic and violent edge to secessionist movements. The lawyers suggest we don't identify which nations are fraudulent scammers, which are nasty white supremacists and which are not quite in keeping with the tone of this book, but don't expect to find the lunatic fringe here.

What you will find are a motley assortment of nations that claim land (even if it's just their own back yards) and have instituted many of the trappings of statehood that we associate with bigger countries. They typically have a flag, a national anthem, currency and stamps. They might even issue passports, grant visas and write and rewrite constitutions.

The selection of micronations here is not exhaustive. Just like real nations, Micronations come and go, albeit at a faster rate. From modern micronational trailblazers such as Prince Leonard's Hutt River Province and the infamous Sealand to recent, highly-developed examples like UK comedian Danny Wallace's nation of Lovely, this is a survey of some of the most active, intriguing and entertaining micronations in the world.

So whether you're a reactionary, a visionary, a prankster, an egomaniac or a gun-toting anti-government conspiracy theorist, there's sure to be something here for you…

And, if you want, this is also a guidebook. Many of the nations included here allow and even encourage visitors. Some even make citizenship available to select applicants (sometimes for a fee). Where possible, we give practical advice on how to get there, and what you'll find when you arrive. This book gives you all you'll need to discover the micronational movement from your armchair or – if you're game – jump on a plane and pay them a visit. Just don't forget to call in advance and let them know you're coming.

If you're lucky, they might put the kettle on.

THE HOW & THE WHO

The Republic of Molossia has a space programme, anti-discrimination legislation and the death penalty. Hutt River and Elleore have universities. Sealand received a diplomatic delegation from Germany. So why aren't these self-declared nations considered 'real'? Or are they? Why aren't they admitted to the UN?

If they have a currency, an official language, an anthem, a flag, a claim on land, a constitution and diplomatic processes, why aren't they invited to sign international protocols? If Vatican City (pop 900), Tuvalu (pop 11,000) and Monaco (pop 32,000) are all countries, then why isn't Lovely, which boasts in excess of 55,000 registered citizens?

According to the 1933 Montevideo Convention on the Rights and Duties of States – a treaty emanating from the Seventh International Conference of American States – a nation needs only four things to exist:

- permanent population;
- defined territory;
- government;
- capacity to enter into relations with the other states.

The convention goes on to claim that statehood is independent of recognition by other nations. In what is known as the Declarative Theory of Statehood, this basically means that if you meet the four criteria, and say you're a country, then you are a country, no matter whether anyone else agrees or not.

Many of the micronations found in this book cite the Montevideo Convention as legal evidence of their legitimacy. Unfortunately for them, the 'legitimate' nations of the world don't care much for the Montevideo Convention. They prefer to work within the rival Constitutive Theory of Statehood. In contrast to the Declarative Theory, the Constitutive Theory posits that a nation has to be recognised by a global community to be considered legitimate.

Take Prince Leonard of the Hutt River Province (see p22). The prince announced his secession from Australia and then declared war. Australian officials ignored him, and certainly found no need to defend themselves. From his farm in the middle of nowhere, Leonard then happily checked off the four requirements to statehood.

- **Permanent population** Sure, Leonard and his family aren't going anywhere.
- **Defined territory** The farm is theirs and has clear boundaries.
- **Government** A system of government has been established.
- **Capacity to enter into relations with the other states** The prince is happy to talk to anyone interested.

According to one interpretation of international convention, the prince wins. The Hutt River Province is a country. But no other recognised nation cares.

This is the great, tragic lesson learned again and again by micronational aspirants: a nation is only recognised as a nation if other nations that have been recognised by other nations recognise it. Got it?

Yes, it's true! It's that random. France? Sure. Taiwan? Sort of, but not really. It's got its own flag and land and a president and it trades with lots of countries, but don't look for its office in the UN building. Palestine?

No, not yet. East Timor? Yes, it's in the club. Somaliland? No. Monaco? Yes. San Marino? Umm…I'll get back to you.

They are a resilient bunch though, these micronational leaders. And rather than swallow this bitter pill of rejection, they spit it out, puff out their chests, straighten the plastic crowns on their heads and just keep proclaiming their independence.

So who are these people? What kind of person wakes up, spits out bitter pills and decides that they're not just a business development manager in Sydney or a school kid in Montreal; they are also a significant figure in world history – the leader of a nation? What kind of person decides that their spare time would be most usefully spent writing a constitution, claiming land, seceding, making up national anthems and awarding knighthoods to their brother?

Lots of people, actually. Admittedly, with very few exceptions, these self-appointed rulers are men…or boys. Not many x-chromosomes in the micronational leadership gang. Of course, the 'official', UN-approved world isn't any different. The greatest number of women ever serving as national leader at the same time was 13, recorded in 2002 and equalled again in 2006. That's less than 7%. For the same well-documented reasons as in the real world – fame, glory, power, control – declaring yourself leader of your own country attracts the gentlemen among us.

Each of the self-appointed leaders in this book has acted for individual reasons. Some have gripes with their government; some just want to have fun; some are trying to prove a point.

And then there are some that just have tax problems.

While there is some money to be made selling coins and passports to collectors and bored eBayers, most people running a country would be happy just keeping the books balanced. Just like the real world.

And also like the real world, there are some people out there not happy with a simple balanced budget. Scams, frauds and other bad behaviour are fairly common in the world of micronationalism. Starting your own country, they figure, is a great way to make a buck.

So as you bravely enter the headspace of our collection of self-appointed rulers, remember to take care, stay alert and keep your credit card securely in your hip pocket.

Part I

Serious
Business

Driven by an intense desire to own part of the world? Wake up in the morning and wonder why you're not a significant world leader with a hotline to the president of the USA? Jacked off at the government and the crappy hand life has dealt you? Want to save the world? Want to see what it's like to have a goat as head of state?

If you answered yes to any of these questions, the following nations might be just your thing. Included in this chapter are some of the most serious, long-lasting and well-developed micronations on the planet. There are a few in here with a legitimate claim to statehood, and their existence is clear evidence of the hypocrisy and impenetrability of the old boys' club of recognised nations.

And then there's the one with the goat.

Principality of Sealand

················· **Motto:** *E Mare Libertas* (**From the Sea, Freedom**) ·················

With one of the more amazing and violent histories in micronational affairs, the Principality of Sealand has been making news on-and-off for four decades. Emerging from Britain's pirate radio boom of the 1960s, Sealand – a crumbling former anti-aircraft tower in the North Sea – has developed into perhaps the world's most intriguing, secretive, disaster-prone and famous micronation.

Despite many claims and scams purporting otherwise (see From the Sea, Freedom, p14), Sealand remains the only operating stationary man-made nation in the world. Something of a living legal test-case for all things sovereign, Sealand draws you in with its bizarre history and keeps you away with its border protection policies.

LOCATION

Sealand is located on an old sea fort (actually an intentionally scuttled Royal Navy barge) in the southern part of the North Sea some 10km off the coast of Britain, near the port of Felixstowe.

FACTS ABOUT SEALAND

POSTAL ADDRESS Sealand 1001, Sealand Post Bag, Felixstowe IP11 9SZ, UK

WEBSITE www.sealandgovt.org

FOUNDED 1967

HEAD OF STATE Prince Roy of Sealand (Due to ill-health, Prince Roy's son, Prince Michael, was appointed prince regent as sovereign *pro tempore* in 1999. Prince Michael is the effective leader.)

LANGUAGE English

CURRENCY Sealand Dollar

AREA Total: 100 sq km. Land: 450 sq metres, about the size of a baseball diamond.

POPULATION Sealand does not release population figures

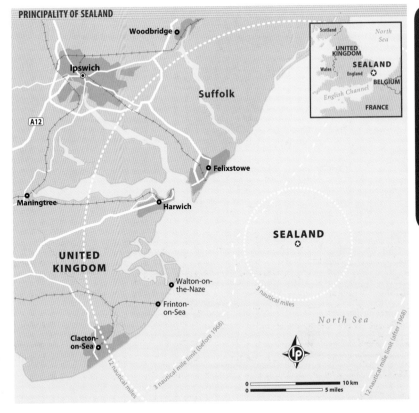

HISTORY

When two British pirate radio station operators stumbled upon the idea of setting up shop on Rough's Tower Gun Platform – a disused military installation in the North Sea – it's a safe bet neither of them would have predicted the amazing events that were to follow.

In the mid-1960s, budding broadcasters were setting up so-called pirate radio stations. Built on boats and marine structures on the fringe of British territorial waters, these stations bypassed British broadcasting regulations and fees. Paddy Roy Bates, who operated the famous Radio Essex and so was already known to authorities, and Ronan O'Rahilly, who operated the pioneer pirate station Radio Caroline, landed on Rough's Tower in 1966.

Along with their radio operations, the two planned to convert the fort into a 'health farm', reportedly to benefit burnt out entertainers. Emerging differences led to a breakdown in the men's business relationship, and Mr Bates seized the tower as his own. O'Rahilly, supported by a small group of men, attempted to storm the base in mid-1967. Bates and his crew were ready; they repelled the attack with guns, petrol bombs and, according to some reports, a flame thrower! Bates then settled on the isolated platform with his wife and family.

Commandos from the British Royal Marines went on alert, and the British authorities ordered Mr Bates to surrender. He refused and, on 2 September 1967, he declared independence for his 'Principality of Sealand'. Warning shots were fired across the bow of a navy ship by Bates' son Michael (reportedly in retaliation for distasteful comments made at the expense of Michael's sister by naval troops).

Following this incident, on one of their regular trips back to England in 1968, Bates and his son were arrested on weapons charges. Surprisingly (and importantly), the court threw the charges out, ruling in November 1968 that Sealand was beyond British territorial control. From this point on, and even following another incident involving the firing of more warning shots in 1990, the British government has largely left Sealand to its own devices.

Through its history, the operations of Sealand have been conducted largely beneath a veil of secrecy. In the first half of the 1970s, Prince Roy oversaw the development of the Principality of Sealand's flag, currency, coat of arms and stamp issues. In September 1975 he declared the Constitution of Sealand, and issued passports to those who had been instrumental in its establishment.

Three years later, Sealand was again in the news after it became the subject of an attack on its sovereign territory by a number of men from Germany and the Netherlands. The invaders, including one Sealand insider, were taken prisoner, but later released following diplomatic negotiations (see The *Other* Sealand, opposite).

During the Falkland Islands war in 1982, rumours abounded that a group from Argentina was negotiating to buy Sealand. Apparently, Prince Roy refused to sell. The next threat to Sealand's independence came in October 1987 with the extension by Britain of its territorial waters from three to 12 nautical miles. At about six nautical miles out, Sealand saw the threat and countered it by simultaneously extending its own claim to 12 nautical miles. According to the official history of Sealand, 'Britain has no more right to Sealand's territory than Sealand has to the territory of the British coastline that falls within its claimed 12-nautical-mile arc'.

Prince Roy – now in his 80s – spends most of his time living in England, after handing effective control to his son Prince Michael in 1999. In that same year, Michael also returned to his house on the British mainland. Early in the new century, the

HELICOPTER IS THE MOST COMFORTABLE MEANS OF REACHING SEALAND

THE *OTHER* SEALAND

One day in 1978, with Roy Bates away from his nation, Sealand's 'prime minister', Professor AG Achenbach, attempted a coup. Backed by some Dutch conspirators, they captured Sealand, and held Roy's son Prince Michael hostage for several days. Achenbach claimed to have acted on the belief that Prince Roy was negotiating to sell the principality. Gathering a small band of armed supporters and a helicopter, Prince Roy retook Sealand a couple of days later (in some reports, the helicopter was piloted by a former James Bond stuntman!). The coup members were held captive, but then – in accordance with international law – the Dutch ring-ins were released upon cessation of hostilities.

It was a different story for Achenbach, who, as a citizen of Sealand, was charged with treason. Pleas to Britain from the governments of the Netherlands and West Germany fell on deaf ears, with the British recalling the 1968 decision that apparently rendered Sealand outside its jurisdiction. When West Germany sent a diplomat to Sealand to successfully lobby for the release of Achenbach, Prince Roy saw the bright side: by sending an official mission, the German government had recognised Sealand as an independent nation (the Germans, of course, have other views).

This might have ended the matter were it not for Professor Achenbach's move to establish a government-in-exile. If the occupying government of the Bates' Sealand wasn't strange enough, the exiled version is positively kooky. Their website (www.principality-of-sealand.de) mentions the missing treasure of the Amber Room looted by the Nazis, contracts with the Soviet army and a secret, mysterious piece of technology called the Sealand Implosion Generator, which the government-in-exile promises to share with any nation that recognises them officially. No takers yet.

Other groups have also traded off the Sealand name. A group based in Spain were printing and selling passports to Sealand in huge quantities. The existence of many thousands of passports was always of concern to the Bates family (who claim to have never authorised the sale of such documents), and when a Sealand passport was associated with the murderer of Italian fashion giant Gianni Versace in 1997, Prince Roy revoked all passports previously issued by his nation.

government of Sealand made an audacious, highly publicised and apparently doomed commercial arrangement with a web-hosting company, HavenCo.

Taking advantage of minimal governmental interference on Sealand, HavenCo aimed to host websites that were too controversial for more compromised nations, such as those promoting Internet gambling, and even the official site of the Tibetan government-in-exile. In the past couple of years, it appears that HavenCo has essentially wound up its operations, following cash-flow issues and a breakdown in the company's relationship with Michael Bates.

In 2004 Sealand announced the formation of the Royal Bank of Sealand, operated from an office in Geneva, Switzerland. It is yet to be seen whether this venture will be more successful than other recent attempts at economic stability.

ECONOMY

There have been numerous proposals to secure the economic livelihood of Sealand since its formation in the late 1960s. Plans have included a 'place for fun', a pirate

ROY AND JOAN OF SEALAND

radio station, a rest-and-recreation centre, maritime radio and various other schemes. Stamps and coins were available to collectors, and were particularly successful in the first decade of Sealand's existence. Through the 1980s and '90s, however, Sealand struggled to gain a firm economic foothold on its Thames Estuary seabed.

HAVENCO

It started as a glorious dream, and offered crumbling Sealand the chance of financial prosperity. HavenCo, an organisation of libertarian dot-com-bubble cybergeeks, struck up a relationship with Prince Michael (Prince Roy, apparently, was not so keen), proposing to use Sealand as an Internet hosting centre. The drawcard was Sealand's independent stance, pirate radio beginnings and disdain for government regulation.

Splashed liberally around the IT media in 2000, the launch of HavenCo on Sealand promised to allow high-security 'colocation' hosting services. The idea was that a company could house their hardware and data on Sealand, thus avoiding any prickly regulations imposed by their home countries. Only a couple of things were not permissible: spam and child pornography. HavenCo was to be the Swiss bank of the Net world.

Only it never really turned out that way. While HavenCo did have some clients and did manage data (gambling sites were especially popular), according to former HavenCo founder and director Ryan Lackey the operation was plagued by unfulfilled promises and high costs. Perhaps most damaging, though, was the too-close relationship between the operators of HavenCo and Prince Michael.

After being appointed CEO of HavenCo, Prince Michael began to impose his will on the hard-line libertarian policies of the HavenCo data experts. According to Lackey, the prince's plans to tax customers and a policy of working with other governments on cyber-terrorism after the World Trade Centre attacks in September 2001 flew in the face of the anti-establishment HavenCo philosophy.

Ryan Lackey, evidently stung by his experience with the company, believes that HavenCo was doomed due to interference by the Sealand government. Sealand didn't even support the proposed development of an online currency.

In the clarity of hindsight, these disputes were perhaps predictable: Sealand has always been striving for international recognition and legitimacy, while HavenCo relied on Sealand remaining a global outsider. Another HavenCo director, Sean Hastings, has continued to live the libertarian dream by becoming involved in plans to build floating communities (see From the Sea, Freedom, p14).

In the late 1990s, the future of Sealand was in doubt, but when web-hosting organisation HavenCo chose Sealand as its operational base, the economic viability of the nation started looking up. HavenCo – a data haven – soon ran into trouble, both financial and, ironically, from the government of Sealand (see HavenCo, above). HavenCo appears to be no longer operating, and with its demise goes much of the hope for a prosperous Sealand future.

GETTING THERE & AWAY

Transport to Sealand is a tricky thing. There are no regular scheduled services, and arriving unannounced can be seriously detrimental to your health. Just ask the British navy!

On 1 February 2002, Sealand suspended its visa program, meaning that no travellers are granted visitation rights. The vague reason for this change of policy was 'the current international situation and other

PRINCE ROY AND PRINCESS JOAN SHORTLY AFTER TAKING POSSESSION OF SEALAND IN THE LATE 1960S

ARRIVAL LOUNGE, SEALAND

factors', although the gradual decline of their one-and-only tenant HavenCo and ongoing economic and political uncertainty would surely have contributed to the decision.

Should visits be permitted in the future, the best bet would be to charter a boat from the English port town of Felixstowe Ferry. Once you arrive, be prepared to be winched up to the landing platform.

FROM THE SEA, FREEDOM

Buy land. They've stopped making it.

Mark Twain

Memo: production resuming.

Seasteaders, 2003

Taking their cue from Sealand (p8), others have looked to the ocean and dreamt of creating a floating world, finding a place where they can be free or establishing a real-estate scam. Some of these floating countries may be genuine micronations, but others may only really exist as a large debit on investors' credit cards.

As early as the 1960s, Ernest Hemingway's less-famous brother, Lester, looked to build New Atlantis on a small timber platform in international waters off Jamaica. Damaged by storms and raided by local fishermen, Lester abandoned the idea of a sea-based nation until 1973 when he began promoting an even bigger platform off the Bahamas. Contradictorily called Tierra del Mar (Land of Sea), the platform was never completed.

A slightly more successful project began in 1967 when an Italian engineer constructed a platform about 11km off the coast of Italy in the Adriatic Sea. A year later, he declared independence, naming his new nation Insulo de la Rozoj (Esperanto for Rose Island). The Italian government responded a little more forcefully than the British did with Sealand: it 'invaded', evacuated and then destroyed the platform. Rose Island's government-in-exile responded by issuing a commemorative stamp of the invasion, but has not established another territory.

Clearly platforms were not the way to go. In 1971 a Las Vegas real-estate developer had several barges of sand poured on a reef just off Tonga. The resulting island was christened Minerva with a declaration of independence and self-created currency to prove it. Several other countries in the area were concerned, but Tonga made a formal claim to the islands and sent troops in to pull down the Minerva flag. In 1982 a group of Minervans tried to reclaim the island, but were kicked off the island by Tongan troops just three weeks later. Another government-in-exile (www.minervanet .org) appeared, with plans to reclaim the island emerging again in 2005.

A more recent attempt aims to create a coral island by anchoring a steel structure in the Saya de Malha Bank of the Indian Ocean. With coral growing at a rate of roughly 2mm a year, it may be some time before the structure is habitable, even by fish. The new nation would be called Autopia, though many believe it will be quickly annexed by nearby Mauritius if the coral does grow into anything that could be considered territory.

As a consequence of Sealand's nation making, the wet-blanket UN Convention of the Sea met in 1982 to look at ways of preventing manmade independent states. The UN ruled that built micronations would fall under the jurisdiction of the nearest country, disappointing a lot of potential micronationalists and creating a lot of business for lawyers into the bargain.

ROSE ISLAND'S FLAG, RECREATED BY THE EMPEROR OF ATLANTIUM (P74) FROM A WRITTEN DESCRIPTION

GEORGE CRUICKSHANK

FROM ROSE ISLAND, MARKED 'ITALIAN MILITARY OCCUPATION'.

FROM THE COLLECTION OF BERNHARD LUERSSEN

Fishing for a loophole in this decree, entrepreneurs looked to create floating nations. After all, if your micronation is under threat from a larger state you can always move somewhere else. One such state is the Principality of New Utopia, the dream of Arizona businessman Lazarus Long (he changed his name from Howard Turney). The proposal is to build a floating nation city about 190km west of the Cayman Islands in the Caribbean, modelled on the European principality Monaco. For the tidy sum of US$25,000, anybody can become a 'Charter Citizen' (apparently only 800 positions are left before their 4100-citizen limit is reached).

In another effort, Norwegian cruise-ship magnate Knut U Kloster Jr began work in 1995 on *The World*, a US$260-million passenger vessel that travels…errr…the world. The massive cruise ship was launched in 2002 and today plies the world's waterways stopping in South America, Asia, Antarctica and several other ports each year. With 110 suites selling at US$2million each, residents are typically multi-millionaires with tax arrangements that fall outside most national boundaries, but *The World* makes no claim to be a country unto itself.

Another super-ship venture, the Freedom Ship, similarly shirks the label of micronation, but shares the same maverick spirit. The project aims to build a ship four times longer than the *Queen Mary* with 25 stories and an airstrip to serve commuter planes. Much like *The World*, this vessel would be subject to the international maritime law and is not a tax dodge, though the aim, according to www.freedomship.com, is to make an 'economically self-sustaining' community. Freedom Ship has been sourcing funds since 1998 and, at the time of research, has still not begun construction.

Another future venture aims to create floating platforms in San Francisco Bay in a development called 'seasteading' or homesteading on the sea. Taking their inspiration from Sealand, a group of computer whiz kids is hoping to build Baystead, a large platform that will have its own solar power and potential for datahaven-style businesses. And according to the **website** (http://seastead .org), 'Seasteading is not just about freedom, it's about freedom, infrastructure, and community united in one place.' It's no wonder that Sean Hastings, formerly a member of Sealand's HavenCo (see Sealand, p12), has been getting excited about the idea of seasteading.

For some the sea is proving to be too difficult and the only way is up. The **Artemis Project** (www .asi.org) is currently looking to colonise the moon by building a base, and are already conducting their first earth-based trials. Sure it might sound like pie in the sky now, but not so long ago people would have said the same thing about a country on an old naval fort.

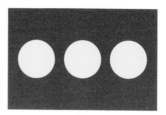

Christiania

CHRISTIANIA

.... **Mottoes:** *Bevar Christiania* (Preserve Christiania); ....
Forsvar Christiania (Defend Christiania)

Every country has its limits; in Christiania it's 'no hard drugs'. As recently as 2004, you could buy hash on the aptly named Pusher St in this little enclave that broke off from Denmark to name itself a 'Freetown' and make its own rules. Current developments by the conservative Danish government are threatening the occupancy of this 'social experiment', which has belonged to Christianites (as locals prefer to be called) for over 30 years.

LOCATION

This fenced-in city occupies prime riverside real estate in the merchant district of Copenhagen, Denmark.

FACTS ABOUT CHRISTIANIA

WEBSITE www.christiania.org

FOUNDED 1971

LANGUAGE Danish

CURRENCY 1 LØN has a value of 50 Danish kroner

AREA 320,000 sq metres

POPULATION 1000

HISTORY

In 1971 a group of Danish squatters founded a nation by breaking into the disused army barracks of Bådsmandsstraede, Copenhagen. Laying claim to barracks and half of Christianshavn's ramparts, the squatters

MOST OF COPENHAGEN'S POST IS DELIVERED COURTESY OF A CHRISTIANIA BIKE

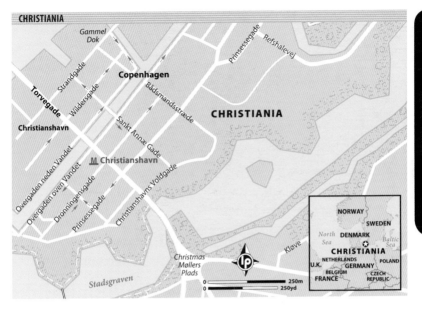

CHRISTIANIA

Gammel
Dok

Copenhagen

Torvegade

Strandgade

Wildersgade

Bådsmandsstræde

Prinsessegade

Refshalevej

CHRISTIANIA

Christianshavn

Sankt Annæ Gade

M Christianshavn

Overgaden neden Vandet

Overgaden oven Vandet

Dronningensgade

Prinsessegade

Christianshavns Voldgade

Christmas
Møllers
Plads

Stadsgraven

Kløve

NORWAY
SWEDEN
North DENMARK
Sea
Baltic
Sea
CHRISTIANIA
NETHERLANDS
U.K. GERMANY POLAND
BELGIUM CZECH
FRANCE REPUBLIC

0   250m
0   250yd

named their territory the Freetown of Christiania, after King Christian, who originally commissioned the military installation.

Despite this show of patriotism, it wasn't long before Christiania found itself in trouble with the Danish government. The liberal attitudes to soft drug use were always going to cause a stir, but Christianites also sought to make their town car-free by barricading streets using rocks. There was a brief period in the 1980s when a bikie gang ran the town, but their reign didn't suit most of the commune. While the Danish government made an initial agreement about the use of the buildings (including a payment of rent), it wasn't until 1987 that the government ruled the town a 'social experiment'. After years of external drug busts, the community worked hard during the 1980s to eliminate hard drugs from Pusher St (see Things to See & Do, p20). With heroin and cocaine out of the picture, it was easy for the Danish parliament to allow Christiania to experiment.

The township prospered as over 70,000 tourists a year came to see the 'Amsterdam of Scandinavia'. The township developed a reputation for culture, and especially for its venues for opera, jazz, film and rock. International guests such as Bob Dylan, Green Day and Rage Against the Machine have all played in the Freetown.

Recently, changes in the Danish government's attitudes to Christiania have seen the Freetown outlawed. In 2004 Denmark abolished its old agreement and sent over 200 police to destroy Pusher St and remove roadblocks. Christianites continued to protest with a large gathering in 2005 attracting 7000 Danes. The future remains unclear with the Danish government's website calling for 'a new development of the area, which accommodates an alternative social structure but according to the general rules of Danish law'.

GEOGRAPHY
Predominantly urban with some excellent green spaces (and not just on Pusher St), much of Christiania is bound either by water or historic walls. There are 15 administrative areas with psychedelic names such as Fredens Ark (Ark of Peace), Psyak (Psychological Action) Area, Mælkevejen (Milky Way), Mælkebøtten (Dandelion), Den Blå Karamel (The Blue Caramel) and Bjørnekloen (Hogweed) Area.

ECONOMY
At first glance, Christiania seems to have a 'bikes and bongs' economy. Tourists come either to gawp at the innovative three-wheel bikes that have become symbolic of the

CHRISTIANIA BIKES

In Copenhagen you can see the unique tricycles delivering the mail, transporting tradesmen's tools and dropping kids off at kindergarten, but outside Denmark the bikes aren't as popular. Peter Santos wants to change that by importing Christiania Bikes into Australia, but has met with a few obstacles. 'They used to have a sticker on the bikes that had "Christiania Bikes.com", Santos says, 'but in Australia everyone is like "Christian Bikes? Christian Bikes? We don't want that!" So I had to take that off.'

Santos' devotion to the machine began when he was a young Dane living in the Freetown. 'I had one of the first bikes ever made back in '82–'83.' When he moved to Australia, he missed them so much that he decided that Australia needed to be one of the nine nations around the world that imports the bikes. Santos rides one himself in his day job as a set designer/builder for a Melbourne-based film company. 'I drive around with my dog and all my tools then I go buy a couple of litres of paint and the dog can still sit there.'

The bikes are still imported from Denmark, though their original creators have moved away from Christiania. According to Santos, 'They became so big that they have to pay tax and have an accountant', though the shop that still sells the majority of the bikes is in Christiania (see Shopping, p20). In Australia **Peter Santos Bikes** (www.psbikes.com.au) sells a few bikes, often to Danish ex-pats, and even had a sale to Micronesia recently. 'I sold two to Guam, because they have a kindergarten for the army base there', Santos smiles.

Unlike most other bikes, Christiania bikes are built to be sturdy rather than lightweight, usually weighing over 30kg. And that's with an empty carrying tray, which can carry up to 100kg, so quick spins are out. 'Basically in Denmark they're made to move kids,' Santos explains, 'but they've made some that you can put a wheelchair in and you can use them as a bridal limousine. They even come as a rickshaw now.'

But it will be a while before petrol-head Australians will see plumbers roll up on a Christiania Bike or leave their cars at home to drop the kids off at school. Santos reckons it's about the expense: 'When it's A$3000, they can go buy a Ford Laser or buy a bike. So it's been an uphill ride.'

alternative lifestyle (see Shopping, p20, and Christiania Bikes, above) or to get a lungful of soft narcotics. But many stop to sample the cafés or go to a gig at one of the many venues in town. Artisans (see Shopping, p20) also do an excellent trade along Pusher St, making local businesses profitable.

Residents pay the Danish government a relatively low monthly rent, which has made the area attractive real estate not just for artists and stoners. Some speculate that recent moves to shut down the Freetown are to allow redevelopment of the inner-city area by large private consortiums.

All residents pay money into the Common Purse, a fund for the community's common expenses that began as a cigar box. In 2004 Christiania's budget was 18 million Danish crowns with a third used for electricity and water, but it has also been used to promote public art and performance.

GOVERNMENT & POLITICS

If you're thinking the only kind of ganja government this freaky Freetown could come up with is anarchy, you'd be very wrong. The basic laws – no cars, no hard drugs, no guns and no stealing – are taken seriously and can lead to expulsion from the community.

With no elected leader, most decisions are made at a Common Meeting with every resident having the right to convene this gathering. Decisions are only made by common consensus, which makes for some long debates trying to get complete agreement. While there are other sub-meetings into building, economy and housing, the Common Meeting decides how to spend the Common Purse and informs residents about relations with the Danish government.

Smaller Area Meetings are held in each geographic area (see Geography, p17) to decide on issues that might occur in individual buildings.

PEOPLE & CULTURE

With just over 1000 permanent residents, Christiania is a large self-sustaining community. The Freetown boasts its own recycling and waste-removal programme, kindergarten, markets and bath house.

There's no doubt that Christiania is the artistic hub of Copenhagen. **Den Grå Hal** (the Grey Hall, p21) regularly features big international stars from Bob Dylan to Blur to Green Day, and provides a stage for local punk, rock and hip-hop artists to cut their teeth. It could be argued that the venue is important to European culture as it hosted the Meeting of Styles graffiti conference in 2003 to the horror of conservative Danish politicians.

But Christianites themselves have a rich creative heritage that began with the Freetown itself. When the government first attempted to oust Christianites they fought back with street theatre protests from the Solvognen (Sun Wagon) group, which has gone on to tour Denmark with its irreverent re-interpretations of traditional Danish legends.

Music is another important protest tool for Christianites, and over the last 30-odd years they've released nine albums, including 2004's *Christiania Forever*. The seminal Danish punk band Sort Sol also formed in Christiania and have been hugely influential on the local scene – a former member even played at the massive wedding of Crown Prince Frederick and the then Mary Donaldson. One successful Christianite hip-hop group, Vote For Truckers, released the single 'Christiania – Hands Off' in the 1990s, which brought more attention to the Freetown. The story of Christiania has been the subject of two recent films Nils Vest's: *Christiania You Have My Heart* (2002) and Christianite Irma Clausen's *Christiania for 30 Years* (2003).

The Freetown broadcasts local music across Copenhagen on its own radio station and a local paper, *Ugespejlet* (Weekly Mirror), updates residents on news from around Denmark.

FACTS FOR THE VISITOR

DOS & DON'TS

In case you missed it, there are no cars, hard drugs or guns allowed here. Locals don't like people taking photos, especially around Pusher St, where you might be mistaken for an undercover narcotics cop.

PLACES TO STAY

There are no places to stay within the Freetown itself, but there's plenty of accommodation in Copenhagen.

PLACES TO EAT

There are several excellent eateries, coffee shops and, ahem, *other* coffee shops around town that offer the best produce in all its forms.

Spiseloppen (☎ 3257 9558; www.spiseloppen.dk; Loppebygningen, Prinsessgade; 5pm-midnight Tue-Sun) Scoring no less than four awards from Copenhagen's *Politiken* newspaper, this is the finest dining you'll find in Freetown – if not Copenhagen – with regular jazz piano tootling in the background.

Cafe Nemoland (☎ 3295 8931; www.nemoland.dk /frame1.html; Bådsmandsstræde 43; ⏰ 10am-2am Sun-Thu, 10am-3.30pm Fri & Sat) One of the nicer spots on Pusher St where you can grab a cold beer to complement your bag of green. The bistro does a great selection of munchies and a small stage hosts regular jam sessions.

Månefiskeren (Moonfisher; ☎ 3257 2708; Fabriksområdet, Bådsmandsstræde; ⏰ 10am-midnight Tue-Thu & Sun, 10am-1am Fri & Sat) Always a little clouded with smoke, this former boilerhouse does good sandwiches, cakes and coffee. It's also the spot for a game of pool.

SHOPPING

Pusher St was once *the* place to buy bongs, papers and other cannabis collectibles. But you can still find fine products in this artsy corner of Copenhagen, especially more imaginative gifts for the folks back home. The preferred unit of exchange is the Løn, though US dollars and Danish crowns are also accepted.

Christiania Bikes (☎ 5696 6700; www.christiania bikes.com; Dammegårdsvej 22) A little difficult to cram into your carry-on, these bikes and trikes have been specially built to transport as much as a car boot in car-less Christiania. If your luggage allowance is stretched, then you can check them out in one of the nine countries that they export to (see Christiania Bikes, p18). You'll see people all over Copenhagen transporting their groceries or kids in these unique bikes.

Women's Smithy (☎ 32 57 76 58; www.kvindes medien.dk; Mælkevejen 83 E) For almost 10 years three women have been hammering away to produce some of the finest metalwork in the city. Their elegant furniture has begun creeping onto society wedding lists with accolades for their sculpture creating a buzz around the forge.

THINGS TO SEE & DO

The easiest way to see what the Freetown has to offer is with a guide from **Rundviser-gruppen** (☎ 3257 9670; www.rundvisergruppen.dk; Gallopperiet, Prinsessegade; tours 30 Danish Crowns), which offers comprehensive rambles in both English and Danish.

PUSHER ST

Once posted with prices for Thai bulbs or Moroccan heads like a produce market, the stalls and card tables of this street have folded up. If you inhale deeply in some of the cafés around the corner, you can still sniff out the earthy smell of hash and residents may sell discreetly along the street. Photography is still forbidden as dealers and locals alike are paranoid about getting caught in a snap that could incriminate them. This place is still a must-see for many

TOTALLY TRIPPY MURAL, MAN

COMMUNAL BACKYARD IN CHRISTIANIA

stoners, but the days of a 'department store of hash' have gone.

PRÆRIEN

Before the creation of Christiania, this large open area was a drill ground, but now it moves to the beat of a different drum. After hash dealers were moved out in 1989, the area was made into a pleasant parkland near the main entrance, which is known for its **farewell sign** 'You are now entering the European Union'.

The nearby **skate ramp** is Copenhagen's first covered space for skaters, including specialised areas designed by local skating company ALIS in Wonderland. It's popular with local and international skaters.

DEN GRÅ HAL (THE GREY HALL)

Christiania's largest **concert hall** (☎ 3254 3135; Refshalevej 2) has hosted a two-day jam for Bob Dylan and, more recently, Denmark's Miss World drag contest dazzled the catwalk. The appeal to rock acts is obvious ('Wanna play in Freetown where dope is freely available?'), but the hall also hosts

theatre, meetings and the annual Christmas knees-up.

OTHER VENUES

It's not all big gigs in Christiania. **Musiklop-pen** (Music Flea; ☎ 3257 8422; www.loppen.dk; Loppe-bygningen; 9pm-2am Wed & Thu, 10pm-2am Fri & Sat) hosts rock from Danish bands and the odd international guest, while **Operaen** (Opera; 1st floor, Pusher St; see posters for details) serves as a centre for jazz, children's theatre and, of course, opera.

GETTING THERE & AWAY

It used to be that you could just follow the aroma of hemp to get yourself to Pusher St, but these days you're better off taking bus No 48 from Copenhagen's Central Station. Alternatively you can take the metro to Christianshavn to walk 250m to the main entrance. Don't be surprised if locals have again rolled stones in front of the entrance to prevent police cars from busting in. There are no visas or other checks at the border.

Hutt River Province Principality

Regarded by some as the world's most established (and lucrative) micronation, the Hutt River Province Principality is something of a template for modern micronationalism. Founded by a disgruntled Australian wheat farmer in 1970, the Hutt River Province has seemingly done it all. Declarations of war, rumours of coups, bad poetry and a curious, quasi-religious obsession with the power of numbers are at the heart of this groundbreaking, desolate province.

In addition to its own remarkable story, Hutt River is also a poster child for the many Australian micronations that sprang up in its shadow (see Mad Aussies, p144).

LOCATION

The Hutt River Province Principality is in Yallabathara, 10km north of Northampton, Western Australia, 595km north of Perth.

FACTS ABOUT THE HUTT RIVER PROVINCE PRINCIPALITY

POSTAL ADDRESS Hutt River Province Principality, PO Box 173, via Northampton, 6535 Western Australia, Australia

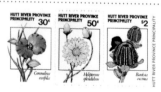

TELEPHONE ☎ 61 8 9936 6035

WEBSITE www.hutt-river-province.com

FOUNDED 1970

HEAD OF STATE His Royal Highness Leonard I and Her Royal Highness Princess Shirley, *Dame of the Rose of Sharon*

CAPITAL Nain

LANGUAGE English

CURRENCY Hutt River Dollar

AREA 75 sq km

POPULATION Although actual residents are very few, the principality claims a worldwide citizenship of 13,000

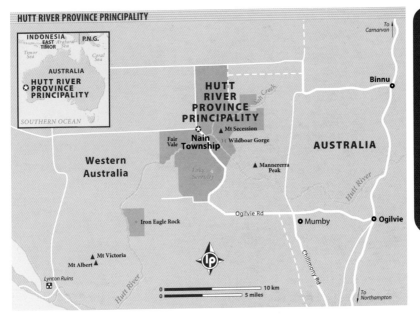

HISTORY

It all started in 1969 with a shift in Australia's agriculture policy. Concerned about an over-supply of wheat, the government announced new restrictions for farmers. Leonard Casley, a farmer from regional Western Australia, was gutted; with thousands of acres of wheat ready to go, he was informed that he was only permitted to produce about 100 acres.

After a failed campaign to change the policy, Mr Casley believed there was only one option open to him: secession. According to an old English law (upon which Australian law is based), the government may not threaten a citizen's livelihood. Mr Casley lodged notice with state and federal authorities on 21 April 1970. According to Australian law, the government had two years from this date in which to protest. Along with their failure to respond came legal status for the Hutt River Province, which was officially a new country on 21 April 1972.

HUTT RIVER POST OFFICE

The following five years saw the emergence of the Hutt River Province's national structures and symbols, including the issuing of coins, banknotes and stamps. The relationship with Australia, however, continued to be difficult. At one point the Australian Postmaster refused to handle outgoing Hutt River mail, forcing it to be diverted via Canada. This philatelic Berlin Wall was just one example of poor relations, prompting Prince Leonard to write the following to Australian authorities in 1976:

I wish that relations between us could be more cordial, after all Hutt River Province is the second largest country in this continent. Australia could be a more neighbourly neighbour.

Ultimately, however, Australia's failure to recognise the Province, along with repeated demands for the payment of taxes, prompted Prince Leonard to take the most drastic of

HIS ROYAL HIGHNESS LEONARD I BUST

actions: he declared war on Australia on 2 December 1977. Ignored again by its massive neighbour, the prince notified Australian authorities of the cessation of hostilities less than a week later. Having actively demonstrated its independence – and in accordance with international law (including the Montevideo Convention on the Rights and Duties of States, 1933) – the Hutt River Province had done all that is required to attain statehood.

Although the political situation in the principality hasn't always been entirely stable (see Kevin the Hutt, left), the nation has benefited from the ongoing leadership of Prince Leonard, who still keeps a tight reign on his nation to this day. And aside from a brief flirtation with the political structure of a 'kingdom' in the early 1980s, the Hutt River Province Principality has remained structurally consistent since its formation.

From disgruntled farmer to national leader, Prince Leonard has certainly made a splash. Like his enormous neighbour, Australia, the prince recognises Queen Elizabeth II. His nation is also deeply religious, with the prince having met Pope John Paul II. According to Prince Leonard, the future of Hutt River is not only assured, it's positively exciting.

ECONOMY

Exports include wildflowers, agricultural produce, stamps and coins. Tourism is increasingly important to the Province's economy.

PEOPLE & CULTURE

EDUCATION

The Hutt River Province has already taken great steps towards establishing itself as a

---

KEVIN THE HUTT

Kevin Gale is part of Hutt River's hidden history. This enigmatic and – by all accounts – charismatic figure from Queensland on Australia's east coast loomed large over the principality in the 1980s.

Mr Gale became a 'Prince Regent' of Hutt River in the early '80s, and worked hard to establish the province's now formidable commercial operations. After a trickle of official stamp and coin releases in the previous decade, Gale oversaw a dramatic increase in printing and minting operations, and also began selling positions within the nobility to interested people around the world.

In the economically heady days of the late '80s and early '90s, Gale operated as a maverick from his Queensland base, capitalising on the fame of the Province, but reportedly operating without the authority of Prince Leonard.

Kevin Gale died unexpectedly in 1995, amid rumours that he and his associates were planning a coup. Some say there was even a plan to relocate the province to an island in the Pacific. He was posthumously declared a traitor.

These events are not included in any official history of the Hutt River Province, and – to this day – Prince Leonard declines to comment.

centre for academic research. While Prince Leonard has signalled his desire to open a university at Hutt River, he is already the founder and trustee of the Royal College of Advanced Research (motto: This We Have Seen and Know).

With a stated mission to 'advance the research and teachings into the fields of Spiritual in relation to pure Physics without relationship to any individual religious doctrine', the Royal College has produced papers written by the prince as well as other Hutt River academics. Vaguely cultish, these articles are based on numerical studies (especially concerning the Christian Bible) and 'wave theory' (see Gematrya Files, p26).

PEERAGE

Hutt River's system of peerage is an essentially patriarchal and hierarchical one. While Prince Leonard still retains ultimate power over each of the Province's three Orders, he has bestowed control on two of his sons. The Royal Order – the most important – is controlled by Prince Leonard's oldest son, Prince Ian. The Serene Order of Leonard is headed up by the younger Prince Wayne.

CITIZENSHIP

As with many emerging nations, the old Australian mantra 'populate or perish' has taken hold in Hutt River. While the prince fixes a visionary stare and speaks of a future in which the Province is home to tens of thousands of people, at the moment he has to console himself with granting citizenship to residents of other countries. Application forms are available on the official Hutt River website.

FACTS FOR THE VISITOR

PLACES TO STAY

Visitors can stay overnight with inexpensive facilities for campers and caravaners, but you do need to take your own food. There are ablution facilities, generated power and limited fresh water available. The Province even offers visitors free use of their private swimming pool! Booking accommodation or a campsite in advance is essential.

PLACES TO EAT

The Hutt River Province has tearooms serving basic refreshments and light snacks. Those intending to stay over should bring their own food.

HIS ROYAL HIGHNESS LEONARD I AND PRINCESS SHIRLEY

SHOPPING

The Hutt River Province Memorabilia Department is responsible for housing and displaying important artefacts from the Province's history. They also operate two gift shops in the Province. Magnets, T-shirts, stickers, commemorative spoons, badges and even a CD recording of the national anthem are all available. *The Man* is the title of an 86-page biography of HRH Prince Leonard, available for A$20.

Many visitors also like to purchase stamps and exchange money.

TOURS

Organised tours to the Hutt River Province from the coastal resort town of Kalbarri are operated by **Kilbarri Coach Tours** (adult/concession/child A$45/42/22; ☯ Mon & Fri from 1pm).

THINGS TO SEE & DO

All of the province's major tourist attractions can be viewed while on an official tour. Ring ahead to check the royals are in residence; you don't want to miss the opportunity of a royal-guided tour. Of particular interest to

ROYAL CAVALCADE

visitors are the **Hutt River Post Office**, the **Secessionist Monument** and the **Chapel of Nain**.

Consisting of over 300 works, the **Royal Art Collection** is on display throughout the official buildings. The collection is viewed during the official tours of the government complex. Of special interest are the Bible-inspired paintings in the chapel. The most appropriate adjective is *unique*.

GETTING THERE & AWAY

A long way from anywhere in particular, Hutt River is nonetheless not too hard to reach. The quickest way from Perth – itself the most remote city in the world – is to fly on Skywest Airlines' daily service to Geraldton. From there, it's only about another 100km to your destination. The drive from Perth takes about six hours; the principality is just off the Brand Hwy.

Once you're on the main highway north of Northampton, turn off at Chilimony Rd. Turn left at Ogilvie Rd. The main border entry is on the right, about 10 minute's drive along the road.

Greyhound and Integrity Coachlines run regular buses between Northampton and Perth and also north to Exmouth and Broome. The trip as far as the Hutt River region takes a bit over eight hours.

Note: the Province is open to international visitors from 9am to 4pm daily.

CUSTOMS & VISAS
For visitors, the Hutt River Province Principality allows entry with a visa (available at the border). Passports are stamped upon entry.

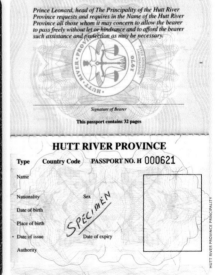

Motto: All Are Welcome, None May Leave!

The shining star of modern micronations is Lovely. The brainchild of British comedian Danny Wallace, the nation of Lovely – centred on Wallace's small flat in the London suburb of Bow – is a compelling emerging nation, a publicity stunt, an idealistic experiment in nationhood and an educational exercise in civics. Described as 'the first fully double-glazed country on earth', Lovely really is quite lovely.

Wallace – aka King Danny I – launched his high-profile nation via a TV series aired on BBC TV in the second half of 2005. *How to Start Your Own Country* was a six-part series that followed Wallace as he went through the process of declaring independence, forming alliances, drafting laws, coming up with a government structure, designing a flag and generally doing all it took to set up his own nation.

As with his previous projects – and especially the book and associated website 'Join Me' (see The Other Lives of King Danny, p30) – Wallace was keen that his new nation was not just an ego-driven gag. He wanted to actually achieve something and, in doing so, has breathed new life into the micronational movement.

LOCATION

Lovely has a small land claim – the flat of King Danny I, which is located in the eastern London suburb of Bow. For security reasons, the precise address of Lovely cannot be made public. This isn't Iceland or the Empire of Atlantium (p74), you know; you can't just knock on the door of the head of state!

Citizens of Lovely are dispersed around the world.

FACTS ABOUT LOVELY

WEBSITE www.citizensrequired.com

FOUNDED 2005

HEAD OF STATE King Danny I (Danny Wallace)

LANGUAGE English

CURRENCY Interdependent Occupational Units (IOU). The Bank of Danny issues IOUs according to the amount of time citizens invest in establishing the nation. IOUs are issued at a rate of one per minute of time invested.

POPULATION Lovely has more citizens than many recognised nations, including Lichtenstein, Monaco and Tuvalu

TIME GMT/UTC

HISTORY

The formation of the nation of Lovely is the most intricately documented of any micronation in the world, covered in a six-part TV series – *How To Start Your Own Country* – first aired on BBC2 in the UK in 2005. Danny Wallace – later King Danny I – commenced his nation-building campaign by exploring territorial options, visiting the micronation of Sealand, invading Eel Pie Island in the Thames near Twickenham, and eventually deciding that his own flat in East London was to become the newest nation in the world.

Wallace then set about bringing together the other prerequisites of nationhood: declaring independence (see Declaration of Independence, right), having a flag designed, recruiting citizens, writing an anthem (see Lovely National Anthem, p31), starting a bank, and – perhaps most important of all – trying to get a song entered in the Eurovision Song Contest ('Stop the Muggin', Start the Huggin'').

Since the TV show first aired, the king has embarked on several more nation-building exercises, including holding a Mr and Miss Lovely competition and awarding honours in the Order of Excellence of King Danny.

CITIZENSHIP & RESIDENCY

While only the kng actually lives in Lovely, citizenship is open to all applicants. Citizens of Lovely are permitted to retain citizenship to other countries. At the time of writing, citizenship applications involved first signing up as a member of the BBC website community.

Citizens are a central plank of King Danny's legitimacy claims. In common with other micronational leaders, he invokes the 1933 Montevideo Convention on the Rights and Duties of States as evidence proving that Lovely is, indeed, a real and operational nation.

DECLARATION OF INDEPENDENCE

An extract from King Danny's Declaration of Independence, sent to British Prime Minister Tony Blair in 2005:

So here we go: I, Danny Wallace, of the address and new country stated above, do hereby declare myself leader of a brand new country, landlocked by Britain, ruled by itself, slave to none other. Phew. There. Said it.

Please do get in touch if there are any legal ramifications to what I'm doing, or if you have any problems with it whatsoever. If you don't ring, I'll just assume everything's a-okay and proceed as planned. Cheers Tony! I'm well up for being allies, by the way!

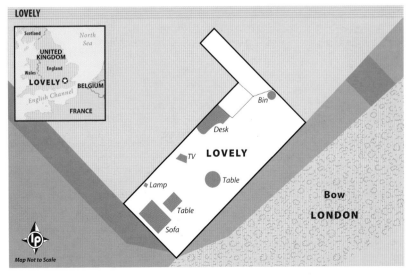

THE OTHER LIVES OF KING DANNY

Before becoming a world leader of considerable significance, Scottish-born Danny Wallace was a comedian and author. Signs emerged, however, that Mr Wallace was destined for more than the limited notoriety garnered by exponents of those noble professions.

First attracting international attention on the comedy circuit with his mate Dave Gorman (they travelled the world looking for other people named Dave Gorman), Danny Wallace took his stunt-focussed brand of reality-comedy to a new level with the 'Join Me' phenomenon.

Creating a global community of 'joinees' dedicated to performing random acts of kindness, and turning it into a best-selling book in the process, Wallace demonstrated his ability to transform comically absurd ideas into comically resonant reality. His ex-girlfriend dubs them 'stupid boy projects', but Wallace's inventive activities often tell us something about being human.

In 2005 Wallace released the book *Yes Man*, describing what happened when he decided to say 'yes' to everything for a year. Lots of credit cards, apparently. He's also recently made a TV show about hoaxes, and a celebrity game show, *School's Out*, where all of the questions are about things the contestants were taught at school. In 2006 Wallace published a book about a manhole cover in Idaho that – according to local residents – is the centre of the universe. If nobody can prove that it *isn't* the centre of the universe…

Wallace must surely be the most diversified, multi-skilled world leader of the past hundred years.

KING DANNY AND HENCHMAN JON BOND ANNOUNCE THE FOUNDING OF LOVELY

PETITIONING THE UN

LOVELY'S NATIONAL ANTHEM

Yesterday was dark and dingy
My temperament was rather whingey
Things had got me wonderin'
Why I lived in London
Anyway – my days were grey

Now I welcome all and sundry
Everyone can join my country
Listen if you're near them
Maybe you can hear them say…

You've got to…
Teach the world to sing
Danny Wallace is the king
For justice and politeness are the laws that
he will bring
Where the order of the crown
Is to frown upon the frown
We done a constitution and we even wrote
it down…

Although the nation may be small
It's the nicest of them all
A land of opportunity
Where crime's against the law
Every subject do your part
With your hand upon your heart
A Kingdom-come-democracy to start…

Everyone is just the same
It doesn't matter who you name
Anyone can be a dame, or sir, or lord
(But not King)
People gather round completely
Listen as I tell you sweetly
All across our nation
Join the recitation with me…

(Followed by general cheering and laughter,
clapping and a joyous jump in the air.)

PEOPLE & CULTURE

The combination of an open-arms policy to new citizens and an active and well-developed online community (citizens are encouraged to interact through online message boards) has allowed Lovely to develop arguably the most active micronational community in the world. In classical democratic style, citizens of Lovely are regularly informed of forthcoming governmental decisions, and are actively encouraged to provide feedback.

As an ongoing social experiment, it's yet to be seen whether the democratic policy of allowing citizens to be so active in the development of Lovely is sustainable. With online forums being what they are, those wanting to contribute in useful ways have to negotiate a vibrant but unfocussed community. A break-away nation or two have already seceded from Lovely. The burning question is, can Wallace's wonderful nation hold it together and become the greatest micronation ever?

LAWS

While still establishing a complete legal framework, Lovely has nevertheless moved quickly to outlaw the private ownership of guns. On the other hand, the right to 'bare arms' is allowed in the summer, especially when it gets hot.

There is no death penalty in Lovely.

RECOGNITION OF NATIONS

King Danny has proclaimed Lovely to be the 194th nation, and is petitioning for membership of the UN. Aside from his own nation, he recognises just one other country not included in the UN: Taiwan. So far, China appears not to mind too much.

PLACES TO EAT & DRINK

Fat Cat Café Bar (☎ 020 8983 4353; Bow Wharf, Grove Rd, Bow) Open all day, the Fat Cat, on the Regents Canal, serves up generous meals at reasonable prices. The food is a mixture of Mediterranean and Asian (with a bit of Mexican for good measure); lunches cost around £8. Enjoy a roast dinner on Sunday.

Kings Arms (☎ 020 8981 1398; 167 Bow Rd, Bow) A comfy, old-style pub with a friendly atmosphere, the Kings Arms attracts locals who like a Guinness, a game of darts and a plate of fish and chips. Honest-to-goodness home-cooked food, a large open fireplace and a pool table cap off the experience. With the gentrification of the neighbourhood continuing apace, the Kings Arms keeps it real.

KING DANNY WELCOMES ALL NEW CITIZENS

King Danny I sent a letter off to the General Secretary of the UN in August 2005, petitioning for membership of that august institution. For the edification of his citizens, the king has outlined the steps necessary to join this most exclusive of clubs:

- accept the obligations of the UN Charter (all 29 chapters of it);
- gain at least nine of 15 votes from members of the Security Council (and avoid the veto votes of any of the five permanent members);
- attract a 'yes' vote from at least two-thirds of the members of the General Assembly;
- pay an administrative 'donation'.

With so many hurdles and hoops to jump over and through, it's little wonder so many other micronations are happy to exist outside this more formal group. Heck, Taiwan isn't a member, and Switzerland only joined in 2002!

Thai Room (☎ 020 8880 6500; G2–G7 Bow Wharf, 221 Grove Rd, Bow) This elegant, authentic Thai restaurant offers a wide selection of tasty dishes, along with a couple of set menu options. Prices match the classy food, although the Sunday lunch buffet is great value at around £8.

Morgan Arms (☎ 020 8980 6389; 43 Morgan St, Bow) On the edge of Tredegar Sq in the less-fashionable part of Bow, this gastropub (named Pub of the Year in 2005 by the *Evening Standard* newspaper) offers fancy fare at fancy prices. Tasty meals come in at around £8 to £10. Drink options include hand-pumped Adnams and Landlord ales. Beautiful!

GETTING THERE & AWAY

CAR
Driving in London? Are you crazy?

AIR
London's Heathrow Airport is one of the world's major hubs for air traffic, servicing over 80 airlines from around the world. It reaches over 200 destinations and sees over 64 million people pass through each year. The Heathrow Express train links the airport to Paddington Station, where a tube train along the Hammersmith and City Line will get you to Bow Rd Station, quite close to Lovely, in about an hour.

TRAIN
To get to Bow from central London, walk east from Trafalgar Sq towards Embankment Pier. You'll reach Charing Cross Station on the Strand after about five minutes. Take the Northern or Bakerloo line to Embankment (about five minutes) and transfer to the District line towards Dagenham East. Bow Rd Station, near the nation of Lovely, is about 20 minutes along this line.

Whangamomona

Based on the Zappa definition (see Introduction, p4), this sleepy little New Zealand town is well on the way to being a country, as it has its own football team and the all-important beer. Set in the North Island's hilly interior, it's the kind of spot where you could film a Kiwi version of *Northern Exposure*, featuring a whole host of quirky local characters against a remote scenic backdrop.

LOCATION

Near the west coast of New Zealand's North Island, a road meanders east of the town of Stratford into the wilderness and the lands of Whangamomona.

FACTS ABOUT WHANGAMOMONA

POSTAL ADDRESS The President of Whangamomona, RD26, Stratford, New Zealand

FOUNDED 1989

HEAD OF STATE President Murt Kennard

LANGUAGE English

NATIONAL DAY Republic Day – held every second year (2007 and 2009 are the next dates), sometime in January

AREA Approximately 1.6 sq km

POPULATION Less than 20 in township

STOP AT THE BORDER (FOR A LOO BREAK)

George Dunford went to Whangamomona for this exclusive in tracky dacks

Before meeting President Murt Kennard I thought it was only fitting to call and make an appointment to see the great man. Fitting into a head of state's diary would be difficult – there'd be budgets to balance, lobby groups to be swindled by and interns to seduce. In Murt's case, he was busy working on an old table in the back shed and confirmed our appointment by saying 'If you turn up, you turn up'.

The current president of Whangamomona could be a bear with a beard. Given that his predecessors were a poodle and a goat (see Government & Politics, p36), I'm lucky he can talk. But he's got nothing but respect for the former leaders. He reckons Tai the poodle had 'a personality of his own. He was a very good president. Every time someone pulled up in town he'd check their car and their tyres out, and them. He'd do a few yaps if they were OK.' When I ask about the state funeral of Billy the goat, there's more than a gleam of sadness in his eyes: 'Well, it was a sad time for us. He was always quiet but he was always there. All his offspring wandered in off the hills for the funeral. And he had quite a family...'

Murt – short for Murtle the Turtle, "cause I'm pretty slow" – makes Whangamomona political history by having the first First Lady. Unlike the other bachelors who have held the office, Murt has Marg by his side to make his leadership a return to family values. Aside from making the famously hefty Whanga burger and playing netball for the Whanga Wasps, Marg runs M&M's café. In between presidential obligations, Murt maintains the town's curvaceous roads and acts as a mechanic. 'Keeping young fellas' cars going while they get a bit of money – most of them still owe me money for it', Murt chuckles.

It was the roads that first brought the motorbiking leader to the town. 'It's an awesome motorbike ride out here! You get to really wear the sides of your tyres out, because you've got corners and good ones. You're on a main highway and you're rattling along and next thing you know you're on 15km/h corners, which is a lot of fun on a big motorcycle', Murt smiles again.

These days he doesn't get out on his old Norton bike as much as he'd like. He's planning to beat the record of the original president, who held office for a decade. The leader is pretty attached to his presidential chain, which is crafted from used beer can tops, local boar tusks, docking rings and what could be orange stones – 'That's for boring meetings', Murt explains then nibbles. 'That's dried fruit.'

His strategy to hang onto the chain in the upcoming 2007 election is simple enough. He reckons he got in 'Just by talking to people and having the luck. All the young 'uns voted for me, because they get to have parties every now and again. I still owe them an election campaign party.' As I'm draining the last of my cup of coffee, I ask if I can have a go of wearing the famous chain. Murt almost growls 'You've got to be voted in to wear it.'

If Murt's winning combination of a laidback attitude and a fierce love of Whangmomona is anything to go by, he'll be wearing it for a lot longer.

HISTORY

If there's one thing you shouldn't do to Kiwis, it's interfere with their rugby. It's a lesson that local councils hadn't learnt when they wanted to redraft local borders to move the hamlet of Whangamomona from the province of Taranaki into the province of Wanganui-Manawatu. After years of playing for Taranaki, Whangamomonans would be asked to play on the same team as their rivals.

After a spirited meeting at Whangamomona Hotel, the townspeople decided to secede from New Zealand and declared themselves a republic in 1989. A president was duly elected (see Government & Politics, p36), and in January of the following year the first Republic Day was held. It continues to be held on odd numbered years.

GEOGRAPHY

Whangamomona is set in the middle of a rugged hilly area, which means roads around the republic twist around tough terrain or in a few points bore right through it. The picturesque tunnels on the road to Taumarunui are engineering masterpieces and tourists stop to photograph them. The rich volcanic soil has created verdant hills and thick scrub.

GOVERNMENT & POLITICS

In its less than 20-year existence, Whangamomona has had a turbulent political history. The president is elected on Republic Day by casting votes into a ceremonial toilet and reigns until the next Republic Day.

The first elected president, Ian 'Kessie' Kjestrup, built the fledgling republic up from nothing and organised the early Republic Days to fund local schools. After almost a decade in office, Kjestrup retired into the hills around Whangamomona, leaving many wondering who could fill his shoes. The elections of 1999 were controversial: a goat, Billy (aka Gumboots), was declared winner. Accusations of vote eating surrounded the hot new president, but he brayed them away with his classic charisma. Many came to regard Billy as a JFK-like figure – true, he had more than one First Lady, but he remained a charming leader, until his career was tragically cut short. At the age of just 14, Billy was taken from Whangamomona in what many believe was an assassination using poison grass. The great goat was buried with full honours on a hillside overlooking his beloved town.

The 2001 presidential race was won by Tai, a poodle owned by Whangamomona Hotel's barman. Tai was known as a great ambassador, frequently sniffing other dogs and making them feel welcome. Ironically, it was this very hospitality that was Tai's undoing as the poodle was attacked by a much larger dog. Much like Ronald Reagan, Tai survived, but many remarked that the dog was mentally scarred by the attack. Retiring early, the dog's owners briefly filled in until the 2005 elections.

Whangamomonans had begun to feel that perhaps animal leaders might not be quite right for the republic. For the first time in history three candidates nominated themselves for election: former President Kjestup, Wellingtonian cross-dresser Bruce/Miriam Collis and local mechanic/roads worker, Murt Kennard. After some heavy campaigning, Kennard was elected president and will stand for election again in 2007.

SPORTS

Rugby is at the heart of Whangamomona's identity and currently there's both a men's and women's team. The netball team, the Whanga Wasps, are feared throughout the Taranaki region. Local sports get a run on Republic Day. Contests including gumboot throwing, whip cracking, possum skinning and horseshoeing are popular with tourists, but the real glory is in the Gutbuster Run. After a crucial warm-up of elbow muscles with a few glasses of Republic Ale, competitors run the steepest ridge in town along a sheep track, all the while followed by a pack of yelping dogs.

The winding narrow roads around Whangamomona are enjoyed by motorcyclists like President Kennard. Other visitors go pig-hunting up in the wild country around town, or take horse-riding treks with local outfit **Over the Top Trax** (☎ 06-762 5544), which can throw in a paddle in a canoe.

BORDER INCURSIONS ARE IRREGULAR, BUT WHANGA IS ALWAYS HOSPITABLE

FACTS FOR THE VISITOR

PLACES TO STAY

There are plenty of rooms at the **Whanga-momona Hotel** (☎ 06-762 5823; 6016 Ohura Rd; d $85), a traditional pub with dinner and breakfast thrown in. You can also get a B&B room with dinner at **M&M's Café** (☎ 06-762 5596; 6023 Ohura Rd; d $75). There's a **motor camp** (☎ 06-762 5881; tent site $10) just outside of camp that also has a large school hall available for larger groups.

PLACES TO EAT

To eat at the president's place, try **M&M's Café** (☎ 06-762 5596; 6023 Ohura Rd; meals $6-12; 🕙 11am-5pm), which does top coffee, cakes and substantial snacks. It's not the Oval Office tearoom, but the US president probably doesn't have Whanga burgers this good hand-made by his First Lady. There's award-winning pub grub at **Whangamomona Hotel** (☎ 06-762 5823; 6016 Ohura Rd; meals $10-15; 🕙 11am-late), plus they pour hefty pints of the Republic Ale.

SHOPPING

Apart from the essential passport (see Getting There & Away, right), there are several other ways to prove your citizenship, including the T-shirt (NZ$30) and the calendar (NZ$5). All available from the pub and café.

On Republic Day the main street is crammed with stalls selling handicrafts and food.

THINGS TO SEE & DO

The biggest day on the Whangamomona calendar is Republic Day, even if it only occurs in odd-numbered years. Townsfolk man stalls up and down the street – many of which are aimed at fleecing the Aucklanders who come in on trains of their last cent. A jester is appointed for the day, and acts as an MC extolling the virtues of the township to visitors.

The main event is the election (see Government & Politics, opposite), with citizens casting their votes into a toilet to show how much they value democracy. Election results are usually in just after lunch, with other activities (see Sports, opposite) keeping the party going until well into the evening.

THE GRAVE OF THE FORMER PRESIDENT AND GOAT, BILLY

There are several pleasant buildings along Whangmomona's main street, many of which have been given 'historic merit' status by the New Zealand Historic Places Trust. The **Post Office** is a good example of local architecture – a weatherboard relic that was built in 1912 and closed down in 1988. **M&M Café** (see Places to Eat, left) is a well-preserved building that originally housed the Bank of Australasia then became the district nurse's residence, before becoming the home of President Kennard.

Across the road the grand old **Whanga-momona Hotel** was where the republic was born over a few drinks. The pub was voted Best Country Hotel in 2003 and 2005 by the Hospitality Association of New Zealand and even has a golf course in its back paddock.

With a trailhead just near the hotel, the **Whangamomona Walk Trail** snakes past the **grave of President Billy** (see Government & Politics, opposite), then up through the Tawa-dominated forest. It's a steep trail that makes for a good half-hour's walk. Another longer walking track follows the old road through **Tahora Scenic Reserve**.

GETTING THERE & AWAY

From Stratford, you can drive east on the appropriately named Forgotten World Hwy to Whangamomona. During independence celebrations, trains run from Auckland to bring in revellers.

Buying a passport (NZ$3) is advised as the border guard has been known to be armed with water pistols.

The Gay & Lesbian Kingdom of the Coral Sea Islands

The Gay and Lesbian Kingdom (GLK) formed in 2004 as a reaction against Australia's decision to ban same-sex marriage. With the charismatic Emperor Dale I at the helm, the GLK claimed the Coral Sea Islands – a cluster of deserted sandbanks off the Queensland coast – as a homeland for gay and lesbian people. Despite internal squabbling that threatened to scupper the entire exercise, the GLK bounced back in 2006 with the announcement of charter-plane services to Cato, the main island.

At this stage, despite questions being raised in rabble-rousing online forums about how the nation would be repopulated for future generations, it looks like the push is still very much on.

LOCATION

In the Coral Sea, northeast of Queensland, Australia.

FACTS ABOUT THE GAY & LESBIAN KINGDOM

WEBSITE www.gayandlesbiankingdom.com

FOUNDED 2004

GOVERNMENT Constitutional Monarchy

HEAD OF STATE Emperor Dale I

CAPITAL Cato Island (Heaven)

LANGUAGE English

NATIONAL ANTHEM 'I Am What I Am' by Gloria Gaynor

NATIONAL DAY 30 August

CURRENCY The Pink Dollar

AREA Total: the GLK also claims the entire Coral Sea Island group (780,000 sq km). Land: 3 sq km (Cato Island).

POPULATION 183 citizens; seven residents

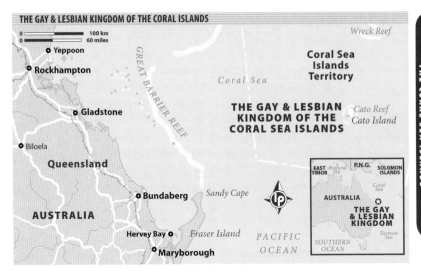

HISTORY

In 2004, when Australia passed laws banning same-sex marriage, a group of gay activists led by Dale Anderson sailed to Cato Island, the largest island of the Coral Sea group, on a boat called the *Gayflower*. On Cato they planted the rainbow flag in protest, thereby declaring the formation of the GLK and the crowning of Dale as Emperor.

Dale's government doesn't mince words; the emperor argues that 'our nation will welcome refugees from around the world like Israel does for Jews' and states that gays in Australia 'live under a system of apartheid' as 'homophobia is nothing less than sexual racism'.

The GLK reckons it has a solid legal backing and intends to take its case to the UN. Dale says that as gays are oppressed and as the Coral Sea Islands are ruled by a 'colonial power' (Australia), then they are entitled to self-determination under the UN's charter, which states that 'an oppressed people ruled by an overseas colonial power shall have the right to self determination'.

In 2005, however, the GLK appeared to be in turmoil. Some websites announced that the emperor had been dethroned; others backed him to the hilt. Others suggested that surely a king should rule a kingdom (or in this case, a queen).

Aside from politics, not everyone has been happy with the GLK's structure. Some lesbians feel under-represented, while some community members believe that bisexuals, transsexuals and transgendered people should also be included in the title (the GLBT Kingdom, perhaps?). Judging by the GLK website, elegibility could simply be a matter of personal taste. With images of pink thongs taking pride of place and a national anthem from disco diva Gloria Gaynor, it remains to be seen whether 'straight acting' gays or 'lipstick lesbians' will get a look in.

EMPEROR DALE IN ALL HIS GLORY

DALE PARKER ANDERSON

39

Still despite what enemies might say, Emperor Dale seems born to rule: he claims he's a descendant of England's gay king, Edward II, and also reckons that one of his forefathers was William Purcell of the HMAV *Bounty*, who in 1789 was the first to visit and live on the Coral Sea Islands.

GEOGRAPHY, WILDLIFE & CLIMATE
The kingdom is pretty much deserted desert islands and coral reefs, and the islands serve as nesting grounds for birds and turtles. In a boon for transgendered people looking for acceptance in the GLK, apparently 90% of all marine creatures in the area change sex at least once in their lifetime.

The weather is tropical, with the occasional thunderstorm.

ECONOMY
Tourism and fishing are mooted as future money-spinners, as is the stock-standard micronational trade: the sale of postage stamps.

PEOPLE & CULTURE
The population is 100% homosexual, so naturally the culture is very gay orientated.

Gay Kingdom
of the Coral Sea €2

Symbols of the Gay Kingdom
Gender Symbols

DALE PARKER ANDERSON

As one article in the gay press lamented, there are no 'trendy nightspots or fashionable boutiques' in the kingdom – yet.

FACTS FOR THE VISITOR

PLACES TO STAY
Camping is free.

THINGS TO SEE & DO

Visit the memorial plaque on Cato, which declares: 'On the 14th day of June 2004, at this highest point in the Coral Sea, Emperor Dale Parker Anderson raised the gay rainbow flag and claimed the islands of the Coral Sea in his name as homeland for the gay and lesbian peoples of the world. God Save our King!'

Swimming, reef walking, lagoon snorkelling, fishing, bird-watching, collecting

CATO, CATO: LAND OF THE FREE

DALE PARKER ANDERSON

DALE PARKER ANDERSON

STARTING AGAIN: IT'S BACK TO ZERO FOR THE GLK

seashells and exploring ship wrecks are all government-sanctioned activities.

GETTING THERE & AWAY

The GLK has announced float-plane charter flights to Cato, due to start towards the end of 2006. Contact the charter company

Seair (☎ 61 7 5599 4509; www.seairpacific.com.au; PO Box 348, Runaway Bay, Queensland, Australia) for further information. Flights (55 minutes) leave from Hervey Bay, flying over Fraser Island; to get to Hervey Bay, take a connecting flight from Sydney or Brisbane.

You don't need a visa to visit, although you do need to be gay or lesbian.

Kingdom of Elleore

Prepare yourself for one of the most quirky and complex tales in this book – a story of bizarre synchronicity and more than a little cultish charm.

The Kingdom of Elleore is the oldest modern-day micronation, having been founded in 1944 by a group of Danish schoolteachers (known as the 'Immortals') on the uninhabited island of Elleore. Later, when the Immortals delved into the history of the island, they discovered it had an ancient lineage exactly 1000 years old, dating back to 944 and the settlement of a depleted band of Irish monks. Against the odds, the monks had more than a little in common with the Immortals themselves…

These days Elleore is uninhabited for all but one week a year, when the king and queen invite their devoted citizenry to the island to celebrate the kingdom – and whatever it stands for.

Good luck finding that out, though: the kingdom is pretty much off limits to 'foreigners', although there are ways and means of becoming a citizen – if you're 12 years old (see p47).

LOCATION

In Roskilde Fjord, Denmark.

FACTS ABOUT ELLEORE

WEBSITE www.elleore.dk

FOUNDED 1944

HEAD OF STATE King Leo III

CAPITAL Maglelille

LANGUAGE Interlingua (an international language along the lines of Esperanto, but based on Latin)

CURRENCY leo d'or

AREA 15,000 sq metres

POPULATION 263 registered citizens

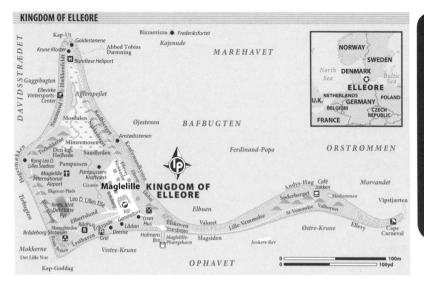

HISTORY

Elleore's history is complex and exists in parallel forms.

First, the pre-history: in 6th-century Ireland, Saint Fintan of Doon founded Clonenagh Monastery. When Fintan died in 603, the monastery continued to operate under his guiding principles. In the 10th century, after persistent harassment from the Roman church, Clonenagh's monks were forced to make their lives elsewhere.

They initially sailed to the Isle of Man before settling on Amitsoq, a tiny island off Greenland's south coast. But the harsh conditions took their toll and many died during the severe Amitsoq winters. The last of the party then sailed south, before extreme weather forced them east – to the Roskilde inlet.

They landed on Elleore on 17 February 944 and immediately fell in love, as the island's landscape reminded them of Ireland in miniature form. One monk declared 'Hic est elie ore!' (Here is the golden island), and the name 'Elleore' was subsequently coined from 'elie ore' (golden island).

The exiles set about building a new monastery, Krune, which was inhabited for a further 600 years. There were more than a few notable monks on Elleore during this time, including the enigmatic Caius (1485–1510), an alchemist and practitioner of black magic who could apparently conjure up storms.

Around the time of the Reformation, the Danes viewed this separate monastic society of Irish renegades with extreme suspicion, eventually attacking the island and burning the monastery down. Surveying the ruins, Oscar, Elleore's last abbot, pronounced that the kingdom would again rise from the ashes, some time in the distant future…

THE ROYAL COUPLE

THE LION, THE DIRECTOR & THE MINISTER OF DEFENCE

In 1907 Elleore became famous as the setting for Denmark's first feature film, *The Lion Hunt*, directed by Ole Olsen. Part of the plot revolved around two fully grown German male lions that kill a goat and an old horse before they, too, are killed by the filmmakers – all of it captured on film. The film created a huge stir in Denmark: Olsen was tried for animal abuse, although he was acquitted, and the minister of justice, PA Alberti, banned the movie from being shown in theatres. This became news worldwide, eventually contributing to Alberti's resignation and the fall of the Danish government (Alberti was already in trouble for large-scale fraud, later receiving an eight-year prison sentence).

To this day there are Elleorians who believe that this controversy led to the Immortals purchasing Elleore, while others reckon it was purely by chance that they came by the island. Whatever the case, the lion is now a symbol of Elleorian culture and can be seen on crests, medals, the coat of arms and all kinds of official documents.

Until then, the surviving monks and nuns had no choice but to go to Denmark and marry into the Danish race.

Fast forward to 1834, when the Danish historian Frederik Barfod helped to found a progressive school for young boys. At this school the teaching was free and the programme subsequently proved to be very successful, so much so that in 1938 the school's language teachers formed a society, Societas Findani, devoted to preservation of the school's underlying philosophy. The society was named after none other than Saint Fintan, who also taught free of charge.

The Findani founders, who came to be known as the Immortals, grew their goals far beyond a mere society – they yearned to form a separatist Findanian state. The first step was to find land, which they did in 1944, in the form of the uninhabited island of Elleore, purchased from a local landowner who had Findanian sympathies. Amazingly the Immortals had no prior knowledge of Elleore's settlement by the disciples of Saint Fintan. It was only later, when they began to research Elleore's history, that they found it was inextricably linked to their sacred saint – Fintan himself.

Like the monks before them, they'd inadvertently found their 'Golden Island' and in 1946 they set about building the castle Braadeborg. However, in yet another vivid echo of the past, this was destroyed in 1958 by 'foreign invaders' (see Geography, Wildlife & Climate, opposite). Thereafter, the people, thoroughly disillusioned, spent their nights in Brinkenborg Castle on the Danish coast and travelled to Elleore by row boat.

In 1963 a full-scale revival of interest saw the purchase of the ship *Løvejagten* and the inauguration of Elleorian Week (see opposite). In 1975 the government purchased a 45-sq-metre tent from a Swedish army depot and anointed it the City Hall of Maglelille.

Now, every year, a newer and bigger tent hosts Elleorian Week and the kingdom is alive once again with rather eccentric people baring their teeth like fangs and curling their hands like claws in imitation of the Lion that Ole Shot, all those years ago... (see The Lion, the Director & the Minister of Defence, above).

A 'KINGDOM OF NO COMPARISON'

GEOGRAPHY, WILDLIFE & CLIMATE

Elleore's shape is approximately triangular, with each side of the triangle roughly 400m in length. The island is flat with small hills, a lake and a little forest. Birds are the only permanent inhabitants (including a large colony of mute swans and a herring gull colony) and the national animal is the lion, a creature that holds a very special place in Elleorian lore (see opposite).

Roskilde Fjord is in fact a bird reserve, which is why the Danish authorities ordered the Elleorians to destroy their castle in 1958 in order to minimise human intervention on Elleore.

The climate of Elleore is similar to the Danish climate. Winter temperatures can reach 0°C; spring temperatures average 10°C to 15°C; summer 20°C to 25°C; and autumn 5°C to 10°C.

ECONOMY

Since 1969 the kingdom has minted coins that have been highly sought after by numismatics. Postage stamps, inevitably, are another sideline.

PROUD CITIZENS DURING ELLEORIAN WEEK

PEOPLE & CULTURE

For most of the year Elleore is uninhabited – except for one week in summer, when hordes of Elleorians descend on the island for **Elleorian Week**. As Elleorians love to say, they are simply returning to their island after 'a 51-week holiday abroad'. During the week the big tent is erected and the City Hall of Maglelille is set in motion. Chefs prepare three-course meals and young Elleorians study at one of three 'Universities of Elleore' and play all manner of games, while the elders get down to earnest historical research or administrative tasks.

Elleorians have a deep respect for the culture of the monks who lived on the island centuries before them. Especially revered are the works of Caspar Tromphett (1583–1653), known as the 'Shakespeare of Elleore' – these days, his plays are performed during Elleorian Week at the ruins of Braadeborg Castle. Another major event

FOR EVERY MAN, A MOTTO

The Immortals proclaimed their first king Erik I, whose motto was 'Let Us Help One Another'. Each subsequent king has had their own motto, including King Leo I ('Seriousness and Merriment'); Erik II ('Faith above Trust'); Leo II ('Hope to the Sea'); and the current king, Leo III ('With Lion and People for the Kingdom'). Erik II's wife, by the way, was known as Queen Lilian the Happy One, leading one to wonder whether Monty Python took Elleore as inspiration for their 'Happy Valley' episode (you know, the one where people who grimace or frown are hanged by the neck until they cheer up).

FURTHER READING

■ *A Kingdom of No Comparison* (1991). This book (a one-off publication, now sold out) took '17 years and three computer systems to finalise' and features pictures and essays written by prominent Elleorians.

■ *The Chronicles of Krune Monastery*. This is a thorough history of the monastery, 'available in every Elleorian bookstore' (wherever they may be – under the Big Tent, perhaps?).

is the **Court Ball**, held annually by the royal couple at Kildegaard Castle in Hellerup, north of Copenhagen, to which all Elleorians are invited.

Elleore's entire population is also enrolled in the air, land and maritime forces, enabling a '300% level of military preparedness' (so they say).

As you would expect from such a disciplined entity, Elleore exacts harsh punishment on anyone who brings the kingdom into disrepute. One of the worst crimes is bringing canned sardines onto the island: apparently it's disrespectful to cram so many 'individuals' into such a tiny space, probably because it's in opposition to what Elleore does with its citizenry. Another no-no is taking the book *Robinson Crusoe* onto Elleore, as the kingdom reckons it gives a 'distorted and false impression of how life is on a small island'.

Elleore officials check all incoming baggage for these items, and if you're found with them the penalty is severe: banishment to the 'prison island' of Kaj Snude, just northeast of Elleore, where you will be required to stand for 11 minutes and 17 seconds. If your crime is against sardines, you will also be required to set them loose in the water.

FACTS FOR THE VISITOR

PLACES TO STAY
Camping is the only option, as there's no electricity or water on the island, but it's illegal to camp without permission (see opposite).

THINGS TO SEE & DO

You can visit the ruins of **Krune Monastery**, or the large stone that was laid when the monks first landed, which is inscribed with the legend, 'Hic est locum' (This is the place). Elleorians call the stone **Anstøds-stenen** (The Stumbling Block) and today it has been moved slightly to the south of its original location for reasons that are not entirely clear.

Fjordmuseet (www.fjordmuseet.dk), a museum in Jyllinge, near Roskilde, contains Elleorian relics.

THE 'GOLDEN ISLAND' – AS SEEN FROM THE AIR

GETTING THERE & AWAY

The state boats *Elfin* and *Sealion* make the journey during Elleorian Week. Note that while only Elleorians have permission to camp on the island, it's forbidden for anyone to land on any of the fjord islands during the bird-breeding period (from 1 April until 15 July).

At any other time Elleore is private property. You might try asking for an appointment to visit, but this is rarely granted to non-Elleorians. If you just want to take a look at the kingdom, try the **Sagafjord boat** (www.sagafjord.dk; adult/child DKK89/39), which travels up and down the fjord – twice past Elleore. During Elleorian Week the islanders salute the boat and the boat salutes them with gunshots. Mind your head.

The other way to visit is to take out citizenship, and that can be done in one of two ways. For the first, you'll need to be 12 and enrolled at Kildegaard School (one of the original schools founded by the Immortals); all Kildegaard 12-year-olds are given the chance to enrol in the Land Forces' Under-graduation Course, effectively an introduction course to Elleorian culture. After that the pupils can decide whether to become citizens or not.

The second way is a bit more accessible: you'll need to be recommended by at least two citizens.

KING LEO III WELCOMES HIS SUBJECTS TO ELLEORE

ORDER OF MALTA

The Sovereign Military Hospitaller Order of St John of Jerusalem of Rhodes and of Malta (known as the 'Order of Malta') is a Catholic order founded in Jerusalem in the 11th century following the first Crusade.

Describing itself as a sovereign state, the order operates from a 6000-sq-m headquarters in the Palazzo di Malta in Rome. Whether this property is sovereign land or not dictates whether the order is a nation or an organisation. There is disagreement on this point, although the order itself maintains that their extraterritorial claim is recognised by the Italian government. One thing is for sure: the order was once an independent state, controlling the island of Rhodes (among other land) for over two hundred years from 1309.

The Order of Malta is a permanent observer at the UN, recognised in the 'entity and intergovernmental organisation' category, along with the likes of the Red Cross, the European Community and Palestine. It is best known as a humanitarian organisation, running hospitals and nursing homes, intervening during conflicts and disasters and operating programmes for victims of disease.

The leader, known as the Prince and Grand Master, is elected for life (much like the Pope). The current leader, His Most Eminent Highness Fra' Andrew Bertie, was elected in 1988. The other four positions in the High Office are the Grand Commander, the Grand Chancellor, the Grand Hospitaller and the Receiver of the Common Treasure. At the 2005 funeral of Pope John Paul II, the Order of Malta's Grand Master was in a position of precedence ahead of Britain's Prince Charles and US President George W Bush.

Akhzivland

Akhzivland is a peaceful anomaly surrounded by the state of Israel. It was formerly the historical village of Akhziv, abandoned after the 1948 War of Independence and later claimed by Eli Avivi, a charismatic ex-sailor who, with his sandals and flowing beard and robes, comes on like a cross between a fit Demis Roussos and the Groovy Guru.

Like Prince Roy of Sealand (p8), President Avivi proved the micronational adage that if you look hard enough, you're bound to find a piece of 'turf' nobody wants. Roy and Avivi also suffered the inverse equation: namely, that once you've got your hands on some idle territory, the bully boys will always try and take it away from you, even if they have no practical use for it.

But like Sealand, Akhzivland refused to give in. It became a beacon of hope for disaffected Israelis, and in the 1970s it embraced the peace-and-love movement and hosted communal festivities and happenings. Today it's beloved of counter-culture freaks and footloose backpackers. They're all attracted to this 'state' that has no real rules and no real government and is guarded by a canine militia.

But so is a very different demographic: newly married couples. For Akhzivland has perhaps the most romantic setting of all micronations, surrounded by mountains, overlooking a beautiful beach, and next door to a national park.

Memo to Prince Roy: that's got to beat an old gun platform in the North Sea.

LOCATION

On Israel's northwestern coast, 4km north of Nahariya.

FACTS ABOUT AKHZIVLAND

POSTAL ADDRESS President Eli Avivi, Akhzivland; PO Box 151, Nahariya, Israel

TELEPHONE ☎ 972 4982 3250

FOUNDED 1952

HEAD OF STATE President Eli Avivi

CAPITAL Akhzivland

LANGUAGES Arabic, English, Farsi, French, German, Hebrew

ALTERNATIVE NAMES Akhzibland; Achsiw; Medinat Achsiv; State of Achziv of Eli Avivi; State of Akhzivland

AREA 10,117 sq metres

POPULATION Two

HISTORY

Before Eli Avivi came to town, the seaside village of Akhziv had a long history, dating back at least 3500 years and changing hands between the Egyptians, the Israelites, the Macedonians, the Assyrians, the Arabs, the Romans, the Ottomans, the Persians and the Greeks.

In 1930, the year Eli Avivi was born, it was part of a British-ruled Palestine, as was Tel Aviv, Avivi's birthplace; as a young man, Eli became a sailor in what he calls the 'Jewish Underground Navy' and ended up smuggling European immigrants into Palestine.

When the British pulled out of Palestine in 1947, the War of Independence between the Arabs and the Jews was sparked off. By the time the smoke had settled and the new state of Israel had emerged, Akhziv's inhabitants had been driven into Lebanon, never to return.

In 1952 Avivi was wandering around Israel. He came across Akhziv, saw that it had been deserted and decided to settle there; the only remaining building was an old Arabic house. From the start, Avivi declared the village to be the independent State of Akhzivland, claiming he was holding the land 'in trust' for its original Palestinian inhabitants. For a while he seemed to be regarded by the Israeli government as a harmless crank and was duly left alone.

But things changed in 1970 when the authorities decided to annex Akhziv into the surrounding national park. When the Israelis sent in bulldozers to flatten the presidential palace, Avivi, according to Akhzivland-watcher SM Pechkin, drew a gun and fended off the machines. He was to be charged with the crime of 'establishing a country without permission', until, says Pechkin, he marched to the capital, charmed the Israeli prime minister, and persuaded the government to lease him the land for 99 years. Another version of the story says that the judge who heard his case sympathised with him and threw the case out of court, ensuring Akhzivland exists in a state of legal limbo to this day.

Throughout the '70s Avivi welcomed all manner of hippies, outsiders, students, artists and misfits to Akhzivland, a motley crew that tended and maintained the land in exchange for food, board and rock concerts.

In the beginning Akhzivland had an agenda (the Palestinian question), although it was never overt and it's not explicitly promoted today. In fact, the president doesn't preach or sermonise; all he has ever seemed to really want is to live a free life, on his own terms, without harming others.

As far as we can tell, Akhzivland transcends issues of nationalism and religion. It's a true Kingdom of the Self and that's enough to warm the cockles of any micronationalist worth their plastic crown and sword.

PRESIDENT AVIVI IN PENSIVE MOOD

ISRAEL TALBY / ISRAELIMAGES

FURTHER READING

- Akhziv (http://pechkin.rinet.ru/foto/il/Asher /Akhziv), a website by SM Pechkin. Features background information and many photos.
- 'A World of His Own' (www.goworldtravel .com), Colin Miller's extensive interview with Eli Avivi, published by the online magazine Go World Travel.

GEOGRAPHY & CLIMATE

Akhzivland is bounded by Lebanese hills in the north, Galilean mountains in the east, the Mediterranean Sea in the west, and the town of Acre in the south.

The area has a Mediterranean climate: hot, dry summers and cool, mild winters.

ECONOMY

Akhzivland's main form of income is tourism, just as well considering the nation's failed building industry (as one recent visitor noted, President Avivi tends to move planks of wood around a lot in order to build platforms that serve no clear purpose and are never used).

The burgeoning worldwide trend in wedding tourism has found a purchase: just-married couples often hire out the presidential villa for photo shoots, although the government has also taken to issuing Akhzivlandian marriage certificates of dubious legality.

PEOPLE & CULTURE

According to SM Pechkin, there's no discrimination in Akhzivland. 'Every nationality is welcome,' he writes, 'except for churls, thieves, cads and misers'. Akhzivlandians are keen amateur historians when they're not diving or fishing. One traveller reports that they also have a passion for nude photography, judging (so our source says) from pictures of the First Lady on the walls of the presidential villa.

FACTS FOR THE VISITOR

PLACES TO STAY

Akhzivland offers a few simple **stone or wood rooms** (per person $34). **Camping** (per night $18) is also permitted. Alternatively, try the **Yad Le-Yad Hostel** (☎ 972 4982 3345; PO Box 169, Nahariya; beds/beach bungalows per person $24/17) in nearby Nahariya.

THINGS TO SEE & DO

The president maintains a small **museum** to house his collection of artefacts from Akhziv's history. Exhibits include pottery and weapons, some obtained during presidential diving exhibitions.

A couple of minutes away, in Israeli territory, **Akhziv Beach** (🕙 8am-7pm summer; admission $3) is a stunning stretch of Mediterranean coast.

WELCOME TO 'ACHZIB LAND': NO MISERS OR CADS ALLOWED

AKHZIVLAND: A LONG WAY FROM THE NORTH SEA...

The **Akhziv National Park** (☎ 972 4982 3263; ☻ 8am-7pm summer; admission $4) has its own sheltered beach and the ruins of a Crusader castle, as well as a restaurant and picnic facilities.

GETTING THERE & AWAY

Take a train or bus to Nahariya via Haifa. There are no visa restrictions.

GAZA DREAMING

In a politically risky move, Prime Minister Ariel Sharon of Israel ordered the withdrawal of the Israeli Defence Forces from the disputed Gaza Strip in August 2005. This move was not popular with many of the Jewish settlers in the area, and few were as annoyed as military historian Arieh Itzhaki. Rather than just accept his fate, pack up and leave, Itzhaki declared his seaside settlement of Shirat Hayam independent from Israel, and named it, with no trace of subtlety, the Independent Jewish Authority in Gaza Beach.

Many locals initially supported Itzhaki, who declared himself the temporary chairman of the new state. The standoff lasted four days. Itzhaki defended his new nation from Israeli soldiers by himself, armed with an M-16 automatic rifle, before finally being evacuated.

Northern Forest Archipelago

Motto: **Wilderness is not a luxury, but a necessity of the human spirit.**

Ed Abbey

Essentially a collection of environmentally-aware citizens who pledge to love and protect the forests of Maine, New York, Vermont and New Hampshire, the Northern Forest Archipelago (NFA) works to love and protect this bio-diverse, sparsely populated region of North America.

The citizens of the Northern Forest Archipelago are not your stereotypical environmental nutters, however. They are committed to spreading the message that the forest is a great place for fun, recreation, tranquillity and beauty, and deserves to be enjoyed, used and supported by all.

The Archipelago exists with three basic principles:

- protect the woods, waters, and wildlife of the Northern Forest;
- promote sustainable use and enjoyment of the woods, waters, and wildlife of the Northern Forest;
- spread the word about the value and beauty of the woods, waters, and wildlife of the Northern Forest, so as to promote and insure their protection over time.

The government of the NFA is a regular participant in micronational affairs and events, and produces and sells stamps and currency. While it asserts a claim to legitimacy as a nation, the Northern Forest Archipelago does not intend to secede from the USA.

LOCATION

The Northern Forest Archipelago is a series of 'islands' of private property and a few claimed parcels of state and federal land in New England's Great Northern Forest in the USA.

FACTS ABOUT THE NFA

WEBSITE http://northern-forest-archipelago.org

FOUNDED 21 September 1998

GOVERNMENT Constitutional monarchy

HEAD OF STATE King James III

CAPITAL Backwoods; located in the Adirondack region of New York State

LANGUAGE English (all forms of communication are respected)

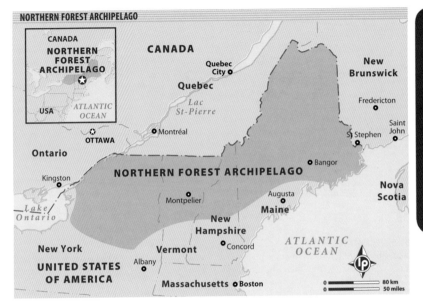

NATIONAL ANTHEM 'Mercy Mercy Me (the Ecology)' by Marvin Gaye

CURRENCY NFA Sweat Equity Buck

AREA 110,000 sq metres

CURRENCY

The NFA Sweat Equity Buck (NFASEB) is a paper-based currency issued by the government and valued by individuals according to their own wants and needs. For labour, NFASEBs are issued at a rate of one per hour. Holders can then exchange them for goods or services. Use of the currency is common among citizens of the Archipelago. Extrapolating from prices for official NFA goods, one Sweet Equity Buck is worth about US$10.

POSTAL SERVICE

The Northern Forest Archipelago has perhaps the most innovative operational postal service in the world. Throughout the Archipelago, a series of Postal Delivery Receptacles (PDR) are available. Mail carrying NFR stamps can be deposited into these boxes, which can be checked by any citizen. If they are travelling near the intended destination of the mail,

Northern Forest Archipelago

First Class Postal Stamp

PLEASING SCENES

they should deliver it. The envelope is then initialled by the recipient. The carrier then takes these envelopes to any government office, and exchanges it for either stamps or Sweat Equity Bucks. Every citizen is therefore a potential postal worker.

CITIZENSHIP

Citizens of the NFA are defined as all living and non-living things residing in land claimed by the NFA. Citizenship is open to any landowner who resides in the Northern Forest region of New England, North America. Applicants must agree to the principles of the NFA.

THINGS TO SEE & DO

APPALACHIAN TRAIL

The Appalachian National Scenic Trail is a wilderness hiking route marked out in the 1920s and '30s. The trail commences in the northeast of the Northern Forest Archipelago in **Baxter State Park**, Maine, and traverses the Northern Forest in New Hampshire, Vermont and Massachusetts before leaving the micronation and continuing through the USA. After 3485km, it finally finishes at Springer Mountain, just north of Atlanta, Georgia.

WHITE MOUNTAIN NATIONAL FOREST

'The Whites' are located in the centre of the US state of New Hampshire, and are an incredibly popular hiking and camping area (receiving more visitors per year than Yosemite and Yellowstone combined!). Wonderfully serviced by a hut system maintained by the Appalachian Mountain Club, the crowds can be avoided if you stray off the Appalachian Trail. Just make sure you can find your way back!

MT WASHINGTON COG RAILWAY

The world's first mountain-climbing cog railway has been ascending New Hampshire's 1917m Mt Washington since 1869. **Mt Washington Cog Railway** (adult/senior/child 4-12yrs/child under 4yrs $57/52/37/free) is one of the region's biggest tourist attractions. From the summit of the mountain, a clear day will afford visitors views of much of the Northern Forest Archipelago (look north), four American states, a Canadian province and the Atlantic Ocean. But even when the view isn't tip-top (Mt Washington has earned the moniker 'home of the world's worst weather'), the experience of riding the railroad on the three-hour round trip is worth the price of the ticket.

There is a gift shop, restaurant and railroad museum at the base of the mountain and the impressive **Sherman Adams Observation Center** at the summit. Bring a jacket, and remember that the train is coal-powered, and coal produces soot!

Mt Washington – along the southern fringe of the Northern Forest Archipelago – is off Route 302 in Bretton Woods, about 260km north of Boston, via Concord. Advance ticket purchases are strongly recommended. From within the USA, call toll-free on ☎ 1-800-922-8825.

ADIRONDACK FOREST PRESERVE

With more than 3200km of marked trails across the 24,000-sq-km Adirondack Park, this is an outward-bound fantasy come true. Just a few hours from New York City,

NATURAL BEAUTY OF THE NFA

the preserve is a unique balance of private and public lands, enshrined in law for over 130 years. Over 130,000 people live in the area, with regulations protecting the natural environment.

Popular areas include the Pharaoh Lake and High Peaks Wilderness areas, and no visitor should leave without visiting the fabulous **Adirondack Museum** in Blue Mountain Lake.

LAKE PLACID

Home of the 1932 and 1980 Winter Olympics, Lake Placid is a year-round holiday-makers' area, featuring **hiking**, **skiing**, resorts, shopping and community activities. Alongside the Olympic-standard sporting facilities and vast wilderness areas in all directions, visitors to Lake Placid can enjoy **Highfalls Gorge**, the **Adirondack Scenic Railroad** and even **Santa's Workshop**.

BURLINGTON

The largest urban area in the Northern Forest Archipelago, Burlington sits on the shores of Lake Champlain (western Vermont), just a short drive from the Canadian border. With the University of Vermont's student population and a vibrant cultural and social life, Burlington has a spirited, youthful ambience.

Just south of town in Shelburne, and only one dollar on the Champlain Flyer train, is the unmissable **Shelburne Museum** (US$18 for 2 days), which holds 150,000 works of American arts and crafts in 39 buildings. There's a classic round barn (1901), a railroad station and locomotive (1915), a circus building, a sawmill (1786), a lighthouse (1871) and even the 1906 sidewheeler SS *Ticonderoga*.

GETTING THERE & AWAY

Perched as it is, less than a day's drive from a quarter of the population of the US (not to mention Montreal, Toronto and Quebec City in Canada), the Northern Forest Archipelago is within easy reach of the world. With the massive international hub of New York City only three-and-a-half hours away by car from the entry town of Sarasota Springs – and Amtrak's *Adirondack* stopping at several Northern Forest locations on its way to Montreal – it's a walk in the park to reach this pocket of paradise.

SEBORGA: THIS ONE'S FOR REAL

The picturesque village of Seborga, located in the Italian Alps near the French border, is one of those many micronations that might very well have a legitimate claim to independence. Seborga hopes to emulate political entities such as San Marino, also bordered by Italy, which operates autonomously from its powerful neighbour.

The 4-sq-km city-state was founded in 954, existing as an independent principality – some say the first constitutional monarchy in history – until 1729 when it was sold to the king of Sardinia. Claims of independence today spring from evidence that this sale was never officially registered. Additionally, there is no mention of Seborga in Italy's Act of Unification (1861) or in the declaration of the Italian Republic in 1946.

German historian and expert on geographical ephemera Wolfgang Schippke, author of *The Mountain Roads of the Ligurian Coast*, claims that Italian leader Benito Mussolini wrote in 1934 that 'for sure the Principato di Seborga does not belong to Italy'.

In the early 1960s, acting on these historical anomalies, local flower baron Giorgio Carbone renewed the ancient call for independence. Enough of Seborga's several hundred residents were keen enough on reclaiming their historical destiny; they voted Carbone – who became known as Georgio I, Prince of Seborga – head of state. Ruling over a period marked by increased tourism, the prince surprised his citizens by announcing his abdication on 20 January 2006, claiming his nation required 'new energy'. Insiders also speak of a quarrel with the town mayor about the style of new paving around the ancient Cistercians Church of Saint Bernardo! Ahhh, local politics!

Seborga issues visitor passports, stamps and local currency. With the support of the vast majority of its population (in 1994, only four people out of 308 voters didn't support Seborga's constitution), Seborga continues to proudly assert its independence.

Principality of Freedonia

PRINCIPALITY OF FREEDONIA

Motto: *Superibimus!* (We Shall Overcome!)

Freedonia doesn't have any land at the moment, but it is still on the lookout. In the meantime, organisers are doing all they can to establish the guiding principles and structures that will exist as soon as they have a plot of land in which to set up shop. And 'shop' is a pretty good word to use: Freedonia is based on beliefs common to libertarians in the USA – and elsewhere in the world – that people should be free to live as they see fit without interference by 'big government'.

Freedonia (it is unlikely that the founders deliberately named their country after the bankrupt nation at the centre of the 1933 Marx Brothers film *Duck Soup*), a nation that started as a hypothetical political experiment in 1992, has – until recently – been a regular contributor and participant in micronational affairs and, by all accounts, is still actively seeking land to establish its tax-free, business-friendly utopia.

LOCATION

While currently stateless, Freedonia's plans include possible land acquisition in the Caribbean, Africa or Pitcairn Island in the Pacific.

FACTS ABOUT FREEDONIA

POSTAL ADDRESS Embassy of Freedonia, 5102 Academy, #4, Houston, TX, 77005, USA

WEBSITE www.freedonia.org

FOUNDED March 1992

HEAD OF STATE John I, Prince of Freedonia

HISTORY

When just starting high school in Houston, Texas, a young man named John Kyle and a group of friends began to wonder what it would be like to live free. Developing a shared political identity as libertarians, opposed to the overbearing influence of governments in the ordinary lives of citizens, Kyle and his friends founded the Republic of Freedonia as a largely conceptual nation (although they did claim their parents' houses as part of Freedonia in those early days).

Hardly surprising for young boys in their early teen years, one of the principle tenets of Freedonia was, and remains, a belief that governments (and probably parents too) unnecessarily curtail individual freedoms through preventative laws. Freedonians don't believe in a 'nanny state' approach that punishes the entire citizenry by restricting behaviour that hasn't happened yet.

All of the founding members of Freedonia shared power as a kind of oligarchy in the early years. Bit by bit, though, John Kyle – or President John as he was then known – began increasing his personal power base. Removing the other president (there were two initially) was one of the last steps needed to totally consolidate power, and in 1997, Kyle reformed Freedonia as a constitutional monarchy, naming himself Prince John I in the process. He was 18 years old.

A constitution was initially drafted in 1997; however, with more structural changes at a government level taking place, a change was necessary after only three years of its operation.

A revised constitution was ratified in November 2000 – the prince was now at college in Boston – outlining detailed rules covering the governance of the Principality of Freedonia. Sections include a preamble (including a Bill of Rights), articles on issues such as legislative powers, the roles and responsibilities of the prince and prime minister, and regulations for the electory council, voting and referenda, sovereignty and even annexation of other lands by acquisition.

Following a disastrous attempt to acquire land in a largely lawless area of Somalia in Africa (see Search for a State, p58), the Freedonian government (read: Prince John I) went to ground. According to a Spanish-language coin enthusiast's website, Prince John claimed in 2004 that his nation project 'is by no means terminated', although he was taking 'temporary leave' from active development of Freedonia.

PRINCE JOHN I

AWDAL INDEPENDENCE

This is an extract from the amazing Awdal Declaration of Independence from Somalia that was sent to the UN in 1995:

The Awdal Republic that will soon emerge will be democratic, compassionate and civilized. Certainly when we achieve our goal, gone will be the days when the Awdalians were the naked needles that sewed other people's clothes; gone will be the days when our destiny was in unfriendly hands and gone will be the days when we believed blindly in Somali nationalism.

The UN has taken no steps to support this declaration.

Such has been the commitment and longevity of the Freedonia experiment, though, that it seems almost certain the nation will again make a renewed attempt at serious statehood in the near future.

SEARCH FOR A STATE

Since shifting from a conceptual experiment to a nation in search of a state in the late 1990s, Freedonia has pursued several occasionally mysterious avenues to achieving the ultimate goal of sovereign land. Currently, Prince John I claims to be investigating what he calls 'location #2' – an undisclosed area where he hopes to establish an 'embassy/diplomatic complex'. Not exactly the glorious city-state described elsewhere, but certainly a positive start.

It is the ill-fated 'location #1', however, that is perhaps the most interesting and controversial aspect of the whole Freedonia experiment. It has also been suggested that the strange events surrounding this location, revealed to be in northern Somalia, Africa, may go some way to explaining Freedonia's lower profile in micronational affairs over the past year or two.

The story is a confusing jigsaw of fact and supposition, involving a verbal relationship between Freedonia and Awdal Roads Company (ARC), a European-based company (incorporated in Mauritius) looking to establish a foothold in the Awdal region of Somaliland. (Somaliland itself almost qualifies for a listing in this book, although its claims of independence from Somalia – an essentially lawless nation in northeast Africa – are too legitimate for coverage here. The fact that the Awdal region itself petitioned the UN for independence from Somaliland in 1995 only adds to the layers in this tale; see Awdal Independence, left.)

Hoping that the ARC could give Freedonia information about investment opportunities in the area, young Prince John I presumably became increasingly uncomfortable as news of the unfolding situation in Awdal emerged. Working with local leaders and Somaliland officials, the ARC identified a port town – Bol Ado, about 60km from the Djibouti border – as worthy of rehabilitation. The ARC's plan was to improve roads and infrastructure in and around this location. Freedonia was also interested in this port town, seeing it as a possible site for a tax-free haven that would lure international investment. A keen journalist at the time described the plan as a cross between Monte Carlo and Liberia. But negotiations were not going well in Africa.

With various Somali political leaders looking for investment in different locations, the ARC negotiators had a difficult task ahead of them. Apparently the Awdal Roads Company was making great progress when a mysterious fax – reportedly sent by a Somali man living in Canada – arrived in the area. According to reports, the fax claimed to contain two pages from the Freedonia website, stating that the Awdal Roads Company was part of Freedonia and that there was already a deal struck between Freedonia and the local sultan. Prince John maintains these claims were untrue and, to say the least, incendiary.

After reportedly heated meetings with Somaliland officials, the beleaguered ARC men made it to the airport and hurriedly left.

The trouble didn't end there. News spread to the Awdal region, with locals furious that Somaliland officials had scuttled the deal with Awdal Roads Company. The Vice President's car was pelted with stones as he travelled through Awdal on his way home from the meetings. Reports suggest that Somaliland security members fired shots into the crowd. One person was reportedly killed, and several more arrested. Their fates are unknown.

According to Prince John I, future plans for Freedonian development will not be

FREEDONIA'S NATIONAL ANTHEM

When a new nation first arose,
Out of the world's oppressive haze,
There was a sound throughout the land,
A newly freed people sung this phrase:

Oh, Freedonia, Freedonia the land that saves,
Freedonians never shall be slaves.

People less fortunate than we,
Sadly to their governments kneel,
While our nation shines great and free,
A land of solace, land of zeal.

Oh, Freedonia, Freedonia the land that saves,
Freedonians never shall be slaves.

In our majesty we arise,
above the world's oppressive states,
People of earth, open your eyes,
And see that your freedom awaits!

promoted on the nation's website. We can expect more discretion – and possibly less ambition – from the prince in future endeavours.

CITIZENSHIP

Citizenship is freely granted to anyone wishing to become a Freedonian. No charge is levied, and there is no need to prove your libertarian values or credentials. A form can be obtained from the nation's website, or from the Freedonian Embassy in the US.

THE GREAT REPUBLIC OF ROUGH AND READY

In 1850 California was in the grip of gold fever, with towns springing up around successful strikes. The wonderfully named town of Rough and Ready – founded two years earlier – had quickly become a teeming town of prospectors. As with many 'wild west' towns, however, Rough and Ready also suffered from uncontrolled lawlessness.

On 7 April 1850, motivated by the lack of policing and also in protest over a new mining tax, the people of Rough and Ready voted to secede. EF Brundage was elected president, immediately appointing a cabinet. His constitution, known as Brundage's Manifesto, included this declaration:

'We deem it necessary and prudential to withdraw from…the United States of America to form, peacefully if we can, forcibly if we must, the Great Republic of Rough and Ready.'

Some now claim that the new republic's secession papers were lost in the mail en-route to Washington. Whatever the reason, the Great Republic of Rough and Ready existed without government interference for the next couple of months.

In the lead up to US Independence Day on 4 July 1850, however, Rough and Ready townspeople enviously watched neighbouring towns prepare for the celebrations. As an independent country, Rough and Ready couldn't take part! One report even claims that other towns refused to sell liquor to Rough and Ready residents. There was only one remedy…

On 4 July 1850, Rough and Ready's flag was lowered and the Stars and Stripes again hoisted. The Republic was dissolved and festivities proceeded. To this day, locals celebrate the secession on the last Sunday in June each year with a street parade and music.

Rough and Ready is located just west of Grass Valley on the Rough and Ready Hwy, off Hwy 80 between Sacramento, California, and Reno, Nevada.

Part II

My Backyard, My Nation

You know that expression, 'A man's home is his castle'? Well, here's a bunch of people who believe it. Really believe it. The micronations in this section are all about taking personal control. The leaders demonstrate better than any psychiatry text the fine line between self-belief and egomania, and they do it with broad smiles on their faces.

Some nations here are pretty funny. But don't get the impression it's all a big joke. No way. President Kevin Baugh of Molossia, who you will shortly meet, says 'While most micronationalists have a decent sense of humour, we work hard on our projects and take them fairly seriously...'

The embodiment of pure micronational spirit – driven neither by ill will nor insanity – is best represented by the nations you are about to discover and the leaders you now have the privilege to meet.

Republic of Molossia

.... Motto: Nothing Ventured, Nothing Gained ....

The Republic of Molossia is surely the most delightful micronation on earth. While it describes itself as a 'developing country', this republic – surrounded on all sides by Nevada, USA – has a long and fascinating history, an incredibly detailed sense of national culture, and a beautiful insight into the ridiculousness of the modern world.

Formed under the auspices of Article 1 of the UN's International Covenant on Civil and Political Rights, which recognises that all people have the right to self-determination, this Nevada-based republic is a light-hearted antidote to the gun-totin', government-hating secessionists so common to micronations on the North American continent.

LOCATION

Molossia is located in the western US. The Molossian Home Territory (aka Harmony Province) is situated within the boundaries of the state of Nevada, just minutes from the old mining town of Virginia City.

Molossia also lays claim to a smaller Province in California. Desert Homestead Province is near the town of Twentynine

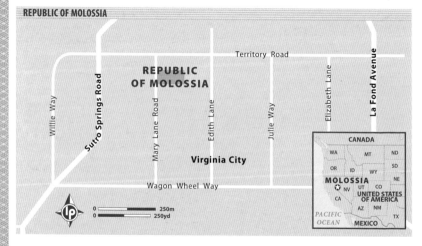

Palms, home to the Joshua Tree National Park and the world's largest marine base.

FACTS ABOUT MOLOSSIA

POSTAL ADDRESS Government of the Republic of Molossia, 226 Mary Lane, Dayton, NV 89403

WEBSITE www.molossia.org

FOUNDED 1977

HEAD OF STATE His Excellency, Kevin Baugh, President of Molossia (b 1962)

CAPITAL Espera, Harmony Province

LANGUAGE English

NATIONAL ANTHEM 'Molossia, Nation in the Desert'

CURRENCY Valora (divided into 100 Futtrus)

AREA Harmony Province: 33,000 sq metres, Desert Homestead Province: 22,000 sq metres

POPULATION Four

TIME GMT minus eight hours, plus 39 minutes, Molossian Standard Time

HISTORY

Note on dates: Molossia has its own system of dates, counting its historical first foundation in 1977 as Year I. For convenience and clarity, we have used both standard and Molossian dates here.

HIS EXCELLENCY, KEVIN BAUGH, PRESIDENT OF MOLOSSIA

Born from the ashes of the Grand Republic of Vuldstein – founded in 1977 by James Spielman (King James I) and Kevin Baugh (prime minister) – Molossia had a difficult birth, taking on several names and several forms over the first two decades (see Birth of a Nation, p65). On 3 September 1999 (XXII) the Republic of Molossia as we now know it was declared, with former prime minister and premier Kevin Baugh taking the helm as president.

Since this time, Molossia has played an unparalleled role in micronational development. In 2000 (XXIII) the Molossian government inaugurated the Intermicronational Olympic movement, and hosted the first Intermicronational Olympic Games. His Excellency won a gold medal in the discus (with Frisbee).

Molossia also spearheaded the movement to have **Norton Day** (8 January), recognised as a global micronationalist holiday to celebrate the memory of Emperor Norton, an eccentric figure who declared himself leader of the USA in 1859 (see Emperor Norton of the USA, p69). Other initiatives of this active nation include the foundation of the annual Norton Awards for Intermicronational Excellence. In 2001 (XXIV), Molossia hosted the showcase Intermicronational World Exposition. Indeed, no other micronation has done so much to encourage and inspire other young nations. His Excellency regularly travels on behalf of his nation, meeting other micronational leaders and forging important treaties.

Molossia's plans for expansion have had mixed results. The beautiful, undeveloped Farfalla Colony was acquired in 2003 (XXVI), and remained a central platform for the nations development capacity until its sale in 2005 (XXVIII). A brief excursion into a second colony, Juniper Hill, was similarly short-lived. Ownership of that land has now reverted to the USA.

In late 2005, following the sad death of the president's father, new territory – the Desert Homestead Province and National Monument – was incorporated into Molossian territory.

With the advent of the Bank of Molossia in 2004 (XXVII) came a maturation of the nation's foreign vision. In contrast with its massive neighbour, Molossia ratified the Kyoto Protocol on Climate Change, signalling the continued thrust of this proud nation into the world spotlight. The Molossian government occasionally publishes commentary on important global events.

PEOPLE & CULTURE

BROOMBALL

Broomball, developed on Molossia's dusty fields, is unique to this tiny nation. It's played with brooms and a ball. It appears that players, often wearing gloves or mittens, have to hit a small soccer ball through makeshift goals. To outsiders unfamiliar with the nuances of this sport, it can appear very similar to field hockey.

SPACE EXPLORATION

In 2003 (XXVI) the Molossian space programme received a boost with the opening of the Rufus T Firefly Memorial National

ALPHONSE SIMMS MEMORIAL COSMODROME AND BROOMBALL FIELD

THE MINISTRY FOR AIR AND SPACE EXPLORATION'S FLAGSHIP CRAFT

Observatory (it's a telescope). The observatory was named to celebrate the Groucho Marx character from the 1933 film *Duck Soup* (Groucho plays the leader of the bankrupt nation of Freedonia). Also in 2003, an attempt was made to launch a probe skywards to provide aerial digital images of the nation. However, the 'Hypérion Balloon Flight and Aerial Survey' was a failure. Despite the use of over 40 balloons strapped to the camera, it got caught in trees.

This was not the first failed attempt at space research. A previous attempt to launch a rocket, the 'Astrocam', resulted only in a damaged rocket and a blurry photograph of land located across the border. It remains a dream of the Molossian space agency to one day obtain aerial photographs of the republic.

LAWS & RULES

Interesting laws and rules in Molossia include obligatory military service, death penalty, free-speech laws and a ban on smoking.

Molossia is very protective of its delicate culture. Citizenship is dependent on full

Founded in 1977 (I), the Grand Republic of Vuldstein was a largely dormant, kingless kingdom for most of its three years, rendered essentially leaderless when King James I moved to a different school. It was renamed the Kingdom of Edelstein and, years later, the Kingdom of Zaria, before becoming the Kingdom of Molossia in 1988 (XI). Led throughout these years by Prime Minister Kevin Baugh (who ruled for some years in exile in Europe), the nation first claimed its current homeland in 1995 (XVIII).

The mid-1990s was a period of power struggles and consolidation in the micronational world, and Molossia – after three months as a provisional communist state – was subsumed as a province of the mighty United Provinces of Utopia. Only months later, the UPOU collapsed, and on 21 February 1999 (XXII) the People's Democratic Republic of Molossia emerged phoenix-like, with Kevin Baugh as premier. Seven months later Molossia was declared a presidential republic, and it has remained so to this day.

residency. Applications for residency are not accepted.

CRIME & THE FENCE INCIDENT OF 2005

Crime is extremely rare in Molossia, but it is not unknown. In late 2005 (XXVIII) a fence was damaged, apparently wilfully. There was no sign that Americans were invading. The Molossian government made the following statement on the incident:

The Americans that live on the other side of that border are notorious drug dealers and users (we are not making this up), a situation that seems to be beyond the control of American law enforcement. Nevertheless, relations between Molossia and 'those people' have been fairly cordial, to avoid any sort of negative behavior, behavior that persons in the drug-dealing business are prone to…

It is presumed that this act was senseless destruction, without any sort of intelligent design. Minor acts of this sort have taken place in the recent past, and have been ignored and quickly repaired. This act of destruction is much more serious, as it will require replacement of that entire section of fence. We will do just that, but take no further action at this time. Nevertheless, the fence will be observed closely for any new signs of vandalism. In case of future aggression, plans are being drawn up for retaliation, by the use of the American legal process, and, perhaps, by other means.

CURRENCY

The Valora is pegged to the value of Pillsbury Cookie Dough, with three Valora being equal to one tube of Cookie Dough.

Currency symbols: Enterprise (Clubs), Strength (Spades), Prosperity (Diamonds) and Happiness (Hearts).

DEFENCE

The army didn't work out so well, and the air force never flew. The navy seems to be the best fit. So, Molossia – a landlocked

DRUG-CRAZED VANDALISM CAUSES FURORE IN MOLOSSIA

HIS EXCELLENCY, THE PRESIDENT, ADMIRAL OF THE MOLOSSIAN NAVY, ABOARD THE MS *WOMBAT*

nation in the desert – has a navy. The navy is proud of its fleet, which consists of the apparently very seaworthy MS *Wombat*.

FACTS FOR THE VISITOR

PLACES TO STAY

While many visitors make a day trip from Reno, Carson City or Lake Tahoe, the closest accommodation is probably the handful of Virginia City options.

Gold Hill Hotel (☎ 775-847-0111; d from $45) South of town on Hwy 342, this has beautiful old rooms.

Crooked House (☎ 775-847-4447; 8 F St; r including breakfast $75-100) Another attractive, lavender-coloured choice.

PLACES TO EAT

Molossia has no food service available. Try the **Mandarin Garden** (30 B St, Virginia City) for affordable, delicious rice plates. Vegetarian-friendly.

SHOPPING

MOLOSSIAN POSTAL SERVICE

As with many micronations, stamps and currency are popular souvenirs for most visitors. Stamp releases include the Marilyn Monroe series, Silent Film Stars series, the Rat Pack series, and a single-release stamp featuring Peter Ustinov.

THINGS TO SEE

MOLOSSIA RAILROAD

With the evocative motto 'Serving Molossia for over a 20th of a century', the Molossia Railroad was opened on 13 March 2000 (XXIII). According to the official history of the railroad, it was 'chartered to run through the province of Harmony, serving the commercial and passenger needs of that province from the Molossian capital of Espera to the German-speaking Molossian town of Steinsdorf'. Thirteen days after commencement, the final section of track was laid, completing 275 (scale) metres of track.

Three years later, an entirely new route was built, with the old lines torn up. This new route runs to 589 (scale) metres. A 390 (scale) metre addition is projected, under the auspices of the yet-to-be-incorporated Molossia Mining Company. Principal locomotive power is provided by a Baldwin 2-4-2 Columbia (Bachmann) engine.

THE PEACE POLE

In a further display of Molossia's broader world view, a Peace Pole was unveiled in May 2005 (XXVIII). There are more than 200,000 Peace Poles in over 180 countries,

ONE OF FIVE LOCOMOTIVES PROVIDING FAST AND EFFICIENT SERVICE IN MOLOSSIA

displaying prayers for peace in eight languages. They serve as constant reminders for us to visualise and pray for world peace.

NORTON PARK

Named after mid-19th-century eccentric Joshua Norton, a San Francisco resident who declared himself Emperor of the United States and Protector of Mexico (see Emperor Norton of the USA, p69), Norton Park is situated out the back of Government House. While it hasn't always been as splendidly attractive as it is now, the park has been a source of considerable pride to Molossians.

Having had a major overhaul in the past couple of years, Norton Park is now an extensive recreational area where Molossians can spend time together and enjoy the outdoors. Features of the park include the **Molossia Railroad**, the **Pineapple Fountain**, and the **Summerhouse**. The expansive **Upper and Lower Plazas** provide a European-style townscape the envy of many cities around the world.

BIJOU THEATRE

Molossia hosts an online cinema, screening the best output from the Molossian film industry. The films – mostly silent – are a combination of drama *(Dastardly Deeds in Dry Gulch)*, nature documentaries *(Wild Weather in Molossia!)* and nation-building propaganda *(A Micronational Award Ceremony,* featuring the former Grand Duke of Westarctica, and *Norton Park Gets a Facelift)*. The films provide a opportunity for people in other countries to gain a glimpse of Molossian landscapes and cultural behaviour. They can be viewed at the Molossian government website.

TOWER OF THE WINDS

Wind is evidently fairly important to Molossians. Like cheese to the French or the steppes to a Mongolian, wind is at the heart of the Molossian national psyche. The following official statement sums up this relationship with one of nature's most powerful forces:

The wind is a part of Molossia, a constant song that plays across the stark, beautiful landscape. It cannot be fought, it cannot be resisted, it must be accepted

and even welcomed, acknowledged as a powerful factor in everyday life here.

The Tower of the Winds is a totemic construction that playfully and poetically references windmills, oil wells and Asian religious rituals. The Tower of the Winds is the unofficial symbol of Molossia, a kind of Stonehenge or Angkor Wat. Kind of. The elements of the tower include the blue Gazing Ball, the Santa Ana Bell and a string of Tibetan prayer flags.

GETTING THERE & AWAY

CAR

Getting to Molossia's Nevada headquarters is fairly simple. From Carson City, Nevada's state capital, it's a 30km car ride northeast along US-50 ('the loneliest road in America'). Head through Dayton and – about 6km or 7km later – take a left at Lafond Ave. Take another left at Wagon Wheel Way and a right just ahead at Mary Lane. The Republic of Molossia is at number 226, just up on the right. Make sure they're expecting you; don't just show up.

AIR

If you're coming straight from Reno/Tahoe International Airport, the republic is about 50km southeast. You'll need to take the 395

THE TOWER OF THE WINDS

THE PINEAPPLE FOUNTAIN AND SUMMERHOUSE

south towards Carson City, and turn off at the Virginia City Hwy. Turn left at the Seven Mile Canyon, just before Virginia City heading for Hwy 79. Fairly quick lefts at Sam Clemens Ave and Sutro Springs Rd are followed by a right at Wagon Wheel Way. Take the second on the left, Mary Lane, and you're there!

TOURS

The government of Molossia only accepts visitors by prior arrangement. *Do not just show up.* Once you've called the government of the Republic of Molossia and made arrangements, plan to spend as much as a whole hour sightseeing. Some visitors have tried to capture the spirit of the Molossian people in only 30 minutes. This package-tour mentality will prevent you from getting a real taste of this unique culture.

EMPEROR NORTON OF THE USA

Emperor Norton I, Emperor of the United States and Protector of Mexico, is a figure who looms large over the history of San Francisco, and also in the hearts of many micronationalists. Molossia, among others, has done much to pay tribute to the memory and legacy of this larger-than-life figure, naming a park in the emperor's honour and establishing the Norton Awards, rewarding service to micronational affairs.

Joshua Norton was born in England in 1819 and travelled widely before settling in San Francisco 30 years later. A leading businessman, Norton was bankrupted following an ambitious attempt to corner the rice market in the gold-rush boom town. Destitute, Norton disappeared for three years, emerging with the following declaration, published on the front page of the *San Francisco Bulletin*:

At the peremptory request of a large majority of the citizens of these United States, I, Joshua Norton, formerly of Algoa Bay, Cape of Good Hope, and now for the past nine years and ten months of San Francisco, California, declare and proclaim myself Emperor of these U.S., and in virtue of the authority thereby in me vested, do hereby order and direct the representatives of the different States of the Union to assemble in the Musical Hall of this city on the 1st day of February next, then and there to make such alterations in the existing laws of the Union as may ameliorate the evils under which the country is laboring, and thereby cause confidence to exist, both at home and abroad, in our stability and integrity.
Norton I
Emperor of the United States
September 17, 1859

For the next 20 years, the emperor walked the streets with his sabre and a cane, dressed always in full – if tatty – military regalia. Locals regularly bowed as they passed, and even the police addressed him as Emperor. He regularly made proclamations, which appeared in local newspapers, including dissolving the US government in 1860, disbanding the Republican and Democratic parties in 1869, and decreeing that a suspension bridge be built from Oakland to San Francisco. When the Bay Bridge was indeed completed in 1936, a plaque was installed at the western end of the bridge in downtown San Francisco:

Pause traveller and be grateful to Norton 1st, Emperor of the United States and Protector of Mexico, 1859–80, whose prophetic wisdom conceived and decreed the bridging of San Francisco Bay, August 18, 1869.

Emperor Norton lived off the generosity of others, a generosity that continued after his death on California St in 1880. His death was front page news – the *San Francisco Chronicle*'s headline was simply 'Le Roi est Mort' (the King is Dead) – and his funeral attracted tens of thousands of people. Despite rumours that he was a rich man, Norton died broke.

In 1990 an opera based on Norton's life was performed, and in 2005 a show called 'Emperor Norton: A New Musical' was produced at San Francisco's Dark Room Theatre.

The Copeman Empire

Ruled by King Nicholas, the empire is actually a small caravan in Sheringham, England; as one of the rare examples of a mobile micronation, the empire is able to tour the UK from time to time and can be distinguished by the 'Monarch on Board' sticker in the rear window. King Nicholas recently published a book regaling the world with his royal adventures, and it's this fact that makes the Copeman Empire a confusing entry in the annals of micronational history.

Is it a joke? A fantasy? An exercise in ego massage? An especial example of whimsical British humour? A particularly clever way for a young jobless guy to make a name for himself? Certainly, the empire shares a lot of similarities with Danny Wallace's Lovely (p28); both kingdoms could be said to be mere sales devices designed to push a product, but in the end, how is this any different than Hutt River selling coins and stamps?

LOCATION

In the Beeston Regis Caravan Park, just outside Sheringham, a seaside town on the north Norfolk coast.

FACTS ABOUT THE COPEMAN EMPIRE

WEBSITE www.kingnicholas.com

FOUNDED 2003

HEAD OF STATE HM King Nicholas I

GOVERNMENT Monarchy

LANGUAGE English

AREA 2.7m wide by 9.1m long

POPULATION One

HISTORY

At the age of 25, Nick Copeman was skint and still living with his mum and dad in Sheringham. With no prospects, he and his mate, 'Baby Face' John Painter, decided it would be a bit of a lark to change their names by deed poll. On a dare they chose royal personas – Henry Michael King Nicholas and the Right Reverend Baby Face Archbishop of Fantaberry – and declared their caravan to be the Copeman Empire. Although Copeman's local dole office was understandably sceptical, the empire gradually gained a cult following to the extent that the king has appeared at the Edinburgh Festival peddling his unique brand

KING NICHOLAS, CHAV SLAYER

of micronationalist fervour. The king has also been known to ride through Sheringham on horseback in full royal regalia, and he once commissioned a private 'royal carriage' on the North Norfolk railway.

As the conclusion of the king's autobiography details, the locals got fed up with his schemes, forcing him to abdicate and sell the original royal seat. However, the king is now back in the throne with a new royal palace – an Eldiss Mistral.

GEOGRAPHY & CLIMATE

The Copeman Empire is a two-berth Eldiss Mistral GTX caravan, with velvet curtains, red carpet, silk trim and a 'throne room' (actually a chemical toilet).

North Norfolk generally experiences its fair share of warm weather. Nevertheless, it is located in England, so the winters can get cold, although we're sure the king will agree to turn up the heating if you ask nicely.

WHY THE LONG FACE, KING NICK?

COPEMAN CROWN COPYRIGHT

such as 'War, Art and the Value of Maize-Based Snacks'. He refers to his mother as 'Mumsy'.

FACTS FOR THE VISITOR

DOS & DON'TS

King Nicholas has made enemies of the local 'chavs' (a term not really translatable from British English, but roughly tantamount to 'roughnecks') who hang around Sheringham. His Majesty styles himself as 'King Nicholas, the Chav Slayer', so make sure you don't take any sides if a skirmish breaks out.

PLACES TO STAY & EAT

The empire exists within a caravan park, so your sleeping options are well defined. As for food, the king likes to make a show of it and eat cucumber sandwiches in public or when receiving guests, as befitting royalty, but most other times the palace is fuelled by

ECONOMY

The empire has a wonky economy. The king has initiated a number of ventures including the sale of peerages on the Internet; forming the King's Trust, which graciously allows his adoring public to help keep him in TV dinners and nice suits; and speculating his dole payments on the stock market.

These days King Nicholas sells knighthoods for a small fee, lives off royalties from his book, and conducts guided tours of the palace. He also takes the palace on the road for summer tours, stopping along the way to allow commoners to enter for £2 a pop. On one memorable occasion, he parked the empire outside Holyrood House Palace, where Prince Philip, it was reported by the local media, was 'quite annoyed' (although a local woman said King Nicholas would make a better royal than Prince Harry).

The empire is also in the throes of developing a sweet-potato crisp range, and there are mutterings about the king's book becoming the subject of a play and a documentary.

PEOPLE & CULTURE

The king is obsessed with marrying Zara Phillips, the daughter of Princess Anne and 11th in the British Order of Succession, although he will settle for a lookalike. He is also fond of giving impromptu speeches,

COPEMAN CROWN COPYRIGHT

THE 'TOURING PALACE' ON A ROYAL TOUR OF THE UK

supermarket 'ready meals' and KFC Zinger burgers.

THINGS TO SEE & DO

Visitors to the Copeman Empire are allowed to take cucumber sandwiches and tea with the king for £1.50. They can also use the palace's 'throne room' for £1.

GETTING THERE & AWAY

Major bus and train lines serve Sheringham from London.

TAKIN' IT GREASY: THE KING REFUELS

Empire of Atlantium

Motto: *E Tenebris Lux* (A Light in the Darkness)

Described as a 'parallel global sovereign state', the Empire of Atlantium is a refreshing antidote to the reactionary self-aggrandisement of so many micronations dotted around the globe. Formed in 1981 by Sydney resident George Cruickshank (then just 14 years old), this 'republican monarchy' is an extremely sophisticated nation-state experiment, as well as an entirely serious claimant to legitimate statehood.

Atlantium advocates progressive, liberal policies, and desires the establishment of a single world government. From its adoption of a decimal calendar to its advocacy of abortion rights and legalised euthanasia, Atlantium is a secular humanist utopia.

LOCATION

While the emperor insists that Atlantium exists primarily by virtue of its global citizenry and governmental institutions, he is nevertheless aware of the requirement for 'legitimate' nations to possess land. The empire therefore lays claim to Emperor George II's 61-sq-metre apartment in the cosmopolitan area of Kings Cross, surrounded on all sides by the city of Sydney. This residence – also the imperial capital – is known as the Imperium Proper. Atlantium's claim on the capital has not been contested by the Australian government, with whom – according to documents from the emperor – Atlantium maintains 'pragmatic, non-confrontational relations'.

FACTS ABOUT ATLANTIUM

ADDRESS 126 Victoria St, Potts Point (the area is commonly known as Kings Cross). Visits are possible only with prior notification.

POSTAL ADDRESS Via PO Box 633, Potts Point, NSW, Australia 1335

WEBSITE www .atlantium.org

FOUNDED 1981

HEAD OF STATE Georgius II, Imperator et Primus Inter Pares (George II, Emperor and First Among Equals)

LANGUAGES Latin and English

CURRENCY Imperial Solidus

POPULATION 903 (2006)

It's interesting to note that Emperor George II rejects the moniker 'micronation'. His ambition is to demonstrate and advocate social change in a style more reminiscent of an NGO.

The emperor prefers to define Atlantium as 'a unique type of transitional progressive political and social group entity that maintains the forms and structures of a sovereign state as a means of giving concrete form to its general ideology, and as a way of wrapping up a diverse range of messages in a form that is more easily understood and digested'.

To spread his message, the emperor is encouraging Atlantium's global representatives to meet with world leaders. In 2005, according to the emperor, Atlantian Legatine representatives were received by the presidents of both Brazil and Venezuela, and by the minister of education of Andhra Pradesh, one of India's largest states, among others.

HISTORY

The rich history of the Empire of Atlantium is commonly divided into two eras.

PRE-REFUNDATIO (1981–90)

Fourteen-year-old George Cruickshank, spurred on by cousins Geoffrey and Claire Duggan (and typical adolescent ideas of liberal pluralism, secular humanism and sustainable globalisation), formed the Empire of Atlantium in 1981. The original 'Provisional Territory' covered just 10 sq metres at that time, located in the southern Sydney suburb of Narwee.

With a constitution based on the 1868 Meiji Constitution of Japan and a bicameral senate in place, elections were first held in 1982. The following four years saw the birth of the Atlantium postal agency, the creation of the flag and other official symbols, and the commencement of relations with other Australian micronations.

Communications between the Hutt River Province (p22) and Rainbow Creek (p145) were cordial, but an approach to the arch-monarchist Province of Bumbunga was met with a hostile response, plunging Atlantium into war. Following the cessation of hostilities (in which Atlantium claimed victory), the Empire of Atlantium adopted a pacifist approach to diplomatic affairs, renouncing its own right to conduct hostilities or maintain any military forces, as outlined in Chapter II of the Atlantian Provisional Constitution.

In 1988, at the completion of Emperor George's university course, most of the citizenry of Atlantium also graduated, creating an inactive diaspora scattered across Australia. The election of Atlantium's third prime minister in 1988 was the last positive action for the decade, followed thereafter by a serious decline in interest and participation from the empire's citizens.

With the official 'Devolution of Authorities' having lapsed following the failure to hold senate elections in 1990, all power was again concentrated in the hands of the emperor. While the empire was dormant for the next decade, it certainly continued to exist.

POST-REFUNDATIO (1999–)

A celebrated event in Atlantium's history occurred on 2 June 1999, when the emperor took legal control of the inner-suburban flat that is now Atlantium's Imperium Proper

EMPEROR GEORGIUS II

and declared the *Refundatio* (or Refoundation) of the empire. Atlantium was back!

Re-energised, the emperor made a series of proclamations, linking Atlantium to its foundations and articulating a vision for its future. Two principles were identified as being central to Atlantium's continued existence:

- that the only demonstrably viable basis for sound, stable, progressive, maximally beneficient government is the recognition that individual rights and collective social responsibilities are intrinsically co-existent;
- that eventual global social, economic and political union is both inevitable and desirable.

A significant policy change saw the empire 'studiously avoiding interactions' with other micronations. The emperor believes that other micronations are 'without exception, wholly inconsequential in the greater scheme of things'.

Two years later saw the commencement of appointments to a transitional government. While all positions were filled at the discretion of the emperor, the gradual increase in government ranks pointed towards the eventual restoration of democracy.

With an increase in media exposure, and an explosion in Atlantium's population (fuelled largely by the Internet), however, no elections have been forthcoming. And while judicial authority has been passed over to a chief justice, there have been no imperial senate sessions for more than 15 years. And while there is a 25-member imperial administration (made up largely of diplomatic representatives and departmental heads), the emperor still rules.

CITIZENSHIP

Applications for citizenship are available and encouraged. Contact the empire or view its website for details. Citizenship is free. Note that, due to 'widespread abuse of the Atlantium Citizenship programme', Nigerian nationals are currently not permitted to apply for citizenship. Unlike most nations, citizenship through filiation is not in force. Children of Atlantium citizens are required to apply for citizenship themselves. Citizenship applications are open to people over 15 years of age.

PASSPORTS

Atlantium believes in the unrestricted freedom of movement for all people and, as such, does not issue passports.

FACTS FOR THE VISITOR

PLACES TO STAY

Accommodation is not available in the Imperium Proper; however, there are hotels and hostels to meet any budget in the immediate vicinity.

EMPEROR GEORGE MEETS PRINCE LEONARD OF THE HUTT RIVER PROVINCE (P22). MUCH TO TALK ABOUT.

Original Backpackers (☎ 02-9356 3232; 160-162 Victoria St, Kings Cross; dm from A$25) Smack dab in the centre of 'the Cross' and set in a wonderful historic mansion, this hostel offers 176 beds, friendly staff, two small kitchens and great outdoor spaces. Free pickup from the airport is on offer.

Victoria Court Hotel (☎ 02-9357 3200; 122-4 Victoria St, Kings Cross; d from A$135) Looking for a quiet, comfortable room with a lovely Victorian air? Try this quaint boutique hotel, directly adjacent to the Imperium Proper, where plush floral-sheeted beds comfort you and in the morning a breakfast buffet is served in the glass-covered patio.

PLACES TO EAT & DRINK

While the Imperium does not have any provision for food service, the streets around offer some of Sydney's best and most diverse dining options.

Jimmy Link's (☎ 02-8354 1400; 188 Victoria St, Kings Cross; mains from A$25) This upscale eatery offers exotic Asian-inspired tapas such as smoked eel in betel leaf ($3.50), while main meals include crispy pork hock, Vietnamese braised Wagyu beef and salmon salad.

Fratelli Paradiso (☎ 02-9357 1744; 12 Challis Ave, Kings Cross) You can have lunch here, and it's great, but what keeps getting us out of bed in the morning is breakfast here. The eggs are magnificent, the rice pudding superb, the coffee from God. Just keep in mind that it closes at 6pm on weekends.

GETTING THERE & AWAY

Citizens and tourists are often granted permission to visit the Imperium Proper. An appointment is required.

Atlantium is located about 1km south of central Sydney. Sydney is Australia's largest city, and is the key international transport hub. Sydney's Kingsford Smith Airport serves over 50 airlines from around the world, including British Airways, United, Air New Zealand and – of course – Qantas. The airport is about 8km from the city, and is well serviced by train, bus and taxi services.

Trains run from the airport to the city every 10 minutes. From there, frequent trains and buses run to Kings Cross; the easiest route to take is the Bondi Junction train or a bus from Circular Quay (routes 324, 325 and 327). Atlantium is on Victoria St.

Kingdom of North Dumpling Island

The Only 100% Science-Literate Society. America Could Learn a Lot From Its Neighbor.

Caption of an aerial photo of North Dumpling in Dean Kamen's office

A genius inventor buys his own island – it sounds like the backstory for a Bond film. It's actually one of the USA's most exclusive micronations. It's closed to the public and visited only occasionally by its owner, Dean Kamen, who invented the Segway human transporter (opposite), but prefers to visit by helicopter.

LOCATION

This small island is in Fisher's Island Sound off the coast of Connecticut, USA, although the island itself is in New York State.

FACTS ABOUT NORTH DUMPLING ISLAND

ADDRESS North of Fisher's Island, Fisher's Island Sound, Suffolk County, NY, USA

FOUNDED 1992

HEAD OF STATE Lord Dumpling Dean Kamen

LANGUAGE English

CURRENCY The Dumpling

AREA 8000 sq metres

HISTORY

When inventor Dean Kamen found himself doing particularly well in the 1990s he did what any self-respecting inventor would do

THE MANOR OF LORD DUMPLING

LORD OF INVENTION

Bestowing the title Lord Dumpling on yourself may not like sound the action of a fully function-ing mind, but Dean Kamen's brain has produced in excess of 150 patented inventions. His father, Jack Kamen, drew for cult comics such as *Weird Science* and *Tales From The Crypt*, but Kamen wasn't inspired by horror-comic mad scientists.

His first invention was a response to a conversation with his brother Barton, a noted pediatric oncologist. Barton couldn't understand why there wasn't a way to give regular doses of drugs to patients, so Kamen invented a portable infusion pump that automatically dispensed medicine with-out the need for regular hospital attention. Based on this invention, he founded his first company, AutoSyringe Inc, at the age of 25.

Medical inventions continued to be important to Kamen and his DEKA company created a compact dialysis machine, a heart stent notably used to patch up Dick Cheney and the IBOT wheelchair-like robot that famously allows users to rise to eye level while still seated in it. Not bad for a guy who failed to graduate from Worchester Polytechnic.

The most anticipated invention of Kamen's career came in 2001 with the release of the Segway. Hyped up to revolutionise personal transport, the device was code-named Ginger and 'IT' with the financial support of Apple's Steve Jobs and Amazon's John Doerr. The two-wheeled machine balanced perfectly and used small amounts of electricity to transport a single person, but just looked, well, a bit geeky. After President George W Bush fell while trying to ride a Segway (some say the machine was off while others blame the tennis racket Bush was carrying), the idiot-proof nature of the invention was in doubt. The machine is used in hospitals and has been spotted around the White House corridors, but the product was only just inside Amazon.com's top 30,000 electronics sellers at the time of research.

Kamen doesn't get to spend much time on North Dumpling, as he's usually travelling to re-search new inventions. His characteristic denim shirts have recently been spotted in Bangladesh, where he's been working on a project to purify water while creating electricity. Called Slingshot, Kamen's latest invention is the size of a washing machine and burns cow dung or any other ma-terial to purify up to 1000L of water a day, while generating a kilowatt of electricity. Potentially, Slingshot could have a greater impact than Segway by balancing health problems in developing nations with their energy needs. It's almost as though Kamen is building a science-fiction utopia his cartoonist father could not imagine.

and went joyriding in his own helicopter. It was on one of these pleasure flights over Fisher's Island Sound that he spotted North Dumpling Island and landed to make the startled owners an offer. The owners were apparently allowed to continue living there, though Kamen began to think of the island as his own retreat.

In 1992 the enterprising Kamen wanted to reduce his power bill by building a wind turbine on the island, but New York State authorities didn't see eye-to-eye with his plans. To build the turbine, Kamen alleg-edly seceded from the USA and signed a non-aggression, mutual-defence pact with his friend (and then president) George Bush Senior. New York State insisted on sending an inspector to investigate the turbine, but the Kingdom of North Dumpling made sure the visit was very much on its terms. The boat transporting the inspector was forced to ask for permission to enter inter-national waters and guns were left on board

as visitors 'to Dumpling could bare legs but couldn't bear arms'. Visas were stamped Dumpling Bozo or Bimbo, depending on gender. When the inspector asked to ex-amine power leads going into the house, Kamen reputedly said it was a Dumpling state secret and the inspector left.

Though Kamen has come to visit the is-land less frequently, the turbine remains powering the island to this day.

GEOGRAPHY

A territory of 200in around the island it-self was established with the constitution, though the local coast guard must maintain the lighthouse, which warns of rough wa-ters surrounding the island.

ECONOMY

The Dumpling is the kingdom's official currency and its value is equivalent to the mathematical value of pi. Kamen is believed to carry several of the bills in his wallet and has been known to use them for payment on the mainland, so some may be in circulation in the USA.

The financial security of the island is based on Kamen's own personal fortune, which – given that he holds 150 patents – must be considerable. According to Kamen, the kingdom's wealth isn't based on the gold standard, preferring the ice cream standard. 'As long as we keep it below 32°F (0°C),' Kamen famously quipped, 'our currency is rock solid'.

GOVERNMENT & POLITICS

Kamen has dubbed himself Lord Dumpling. In his North Dumpling Constitution he appointed friends and family to a variety of offices including the Ministry of Nepotism and the Ministry of Brunch. Perhaps the most important food office created was the Joint Ministries of Ice Cream, for which Kamen recruited none other than ice-cream moguls Ben Cohen and Jerry Greenfield (founders of Ben & Jerry's).

IT TAKES VERY SMALL DRUIDS, BUT NORTH DUMPLING'S STONEHENGE IS FULLY INTERACTIVE

NORTH DUMPLING'S NATIONAL ANTHEM

Kamen famously composed the national anthem to reflect his own tastes and believes it should be sung to the tune of 'America the Beautiful'. According to the biography of Kamen, *Code Name Ginger*, its lyrics are as follows:

North Dum-pling, North Dum-pling,
Keep lawyers far from thee!
And MBAs and bureaucrats,
That we may all be free!

THINGS TO SEE & DO

The closest you can actually get to North Dumpling Island without being a personal pal of Kamen is with a **cruise** around the island. From this vantage you can see the **lighthouse**, which was built in 1849 and reputedly used to signal in booze-bearing boats during the prohibition of the 1930s. Aside from the lighthouse and a roomy residence, the only other notable structure is a **reconstruction of Stonehenge**, which, unlike its *Spinal Tap* counterpart, is in no danger of being squashed by a dwarf.

NORTH DUMPLING FROM A DISTANCE

GETTING THERE & AWAY

Unless you're a New York State inspector or a personal friend of Dean Kamen, North Dumpling is strictly off limits. Pleasure cruises around the island leave from Fisher's Island, but none of these are allowed to land on the island itself. Other than this, you could hang around IT conventions and see if Kamen himself will take you over in his personal helicopter.

As for visa arrangements, the last visa issued was to the New York State inspector who inspected the wind turbine. It was stamped Dumpling Bozo and was on official Dumpling stationary.

EXACTLY THE TYPE

Easily the most famous micronational hoax was the creation of the tiny nation of San Serriffe by Britain's *Guardian* newspaper in 1977. Appearing on April Fool's Day in that and several subsequent years, San Serriffe became a hoax sensation when thousands of readers contacted the paper requesting more details on the country.

Shaped suspiciously like a semi-colon, San Serriffe was purportedly made up of two islands – Upper Caisse and Lower Caisse. In 1999, in a 'Return to San Serriffe' special following the overthrow of the despotic General Pica (written by Berlin Sans), the *Guardian* again fooled thousands of readers.

Republic of Kugelmugel

Kugelmugel is more than a micronation: it's simultaneously a house and a work of art. But it's also a classic illustration of that age-old struggle: One Man against the System. Despite all attempts to squash it, Kugelmugel has endured – and throughout it all, exiled President Edwin Lipburger stands tall as its founder, its head of state, its defence force and its sole citizen. Now 77, President Lipburger lives in Austrian exile, watching as his radical experiment in spherical housing is reappraised and hailed as a masterpiece of micronationalism (and postmodern architecture).

It wasn't always that way. In fact, Kugelmugel used to provoke extreme reactions in the outside world: the republic has been invaded and its population forcibly repatriated twice (shockingly, on one of those occasions every single citizen was imprisoned).

Today Kugelmugel is uninhabited, but you can still visit it and marvel at the sight of its state border, festooned with barbed wire and designer-industrial signage for retro-Berlin thrills.

Best of all, Kugelmugel is round, and as President Lipburger has said all along, 'Round is free'.

LOCATION

Kugelmugel is in the Wiener Prater in Vienna, Austria, a public park in the Leopoldstadt district.

FACTS ABOUT KUGELMUGEL

WEBSITE www.republik-kugelmugel.com

FOUNDED 1984

GOVERNMENT Republic

HEAD OF STATE President Edwin Lipburger

IT ALL BEGAN WITH A VISION

CAPITAL Kugelmugel

LANGUAGE German

AREA 7.68m in diameter

POPULATION One

HISTORY

Before he became president of Kugelmugel, Edwin Lipburger was just an Austrian artist, albeit one with a singular vision. Many artists see themselves as square pegs in round holes, but Lipburger was literally the reverse: he was obsessed with balls and spheres, seeing in them some kind of universal cosmic harmony. 'Everything is round', he wrote. 'The Earth, life, the ball, everything turns... why not live in balls? Round is free, it has no beginning or end.'

Struck by this wisdom, in 1971 Lipburger set about designing a spherical house, which he called Sphaera 2000. The house was to have a diameter of exactly 7.68m and would consist of wood-finished units covered with zinc-coated sheets, bolted with 12mm screws and sealed with permanent elastic.

Lipburger originally built Kugelmugel (it means 'Ball Hill') on a farm in Katzelsdorf, declaring, 'It's hard to hurt the Earth, but it has to be. Ploughing is a genuinely male pursuit. What was down is now above.' However, he was ordered to demolish it by

THE ORIGINAL KUGELMUGEL: ALMOST THERE...

83

the authorities, as the sphere contravened local planning permits, so Lipburger declared the house an independent republic, elected himself president, and began to issue his own stamps and passports.

Kugelmugel began to receive press attention and a steady stream of visitors, but Lipburger was under persistent legal pressure to demolish his republic. In the end he spent 10 weeks in jail and was only released after receiving a pardon from his Austrian counterpart. The Austrian government then seized Kugelmugel and transferred it to the Wiener Prater where it sits today, next to an enormous Ferris wheel and amusement park – the final irony for a man with a reasonably serious mission on his mind.

Even so, the authorities insist on promoting Kugelmugel as a 'state within a state', thereby trading on the micronationalist aspirations of Lipburger's creation, while raking in some tourist cash to boot.

In 2005 the house was the subject of a major exhibition by the Croy Nielsen artistic team (www.croynielsen.de).

GEOGRAPHY & CLIMATE

Kugelmugel has a moderate central European climate. Be prepared for a range of conditions dependent on altitude; if you stand on top of Kugelmugel, closest to the

THE INDEFATIGABLE PRESIDENT EDWIN LIPBURGER

sun, you might suffer some kind of surface glare from the nation's outer shell. The western part of the country is the greenest, with overhanging trees from the surrounding Wiener Prater providing shade and a splash of natural colour. Temperatures in July are above 19°C and annual rainfall is less than 80cm; temperatures fluctuate between 20°C and 25°C in summer, 1°C and 4°C in winter, and 8°C and 15°C in spring and autumn.

OUT OF BOUNDS: KUGELMUGEL TODAY

PEOPLE & CULTURE

The Kugelmugian national psyche is fiercely independent and protective of its identity, but it's also creative – Kugelmugians possess a fiery spirit and a 'never say die' attitude that often channels rage into striking artistic objects.

One hundred per cent of Kugelmugel's population is of Austrian extraction and all Kugelmugians enjoy architecture and philately.

FACTS FOR THE VISITOR

DOS & DON'TS

Kugelmugel's borders are locked, which means you can only observe the nation from Austria. Don't try and climb the fence; you might cut yourself on the barbed wire.

PLACES TO STAY & EAT

Kugelmugel has no hotels or restaurants. Bring a picnic lunch and eat in the Wiener Prater.

THINGS TO SEE & DO

The Wiener Prater includes a large amusement park with a huge Ferris wheel that dominates the skyline and some roller coasters.

The months between December to April should be ideal for skiing, although you'd have to be an A-grade nutter to ski Kugelmugel's spherical surface.

GETTING THERE & AWAY

Take the U-bahn to Praterstern – Wiener Prater is a few minutes away.

GREETINGS FROM KUGELMUGEL: AN OFFICIAL POSTCARD FROM THE GLORY YEARS

Grand Duchy of the Lagoan Isles

Motto: *As Ondas do Amor Cercam-nos*
(The Water of Love Surrounds Us)

The Grand Duchy of the Lagoan Isles is a tiny, tiny nation located within a small spring-fed natural pond about 1km west of Langstone Harbour in Portsmouth, England. Known for at least the past 350 years as Baffins Pond, the grand duchy was founded in 2005 to celebrate the environmental and social gifts the pond offers the local community (and to capitalise on a local council loophole).

Even before the grand duchy turned its attentions to Baffins Pond, it was hardly unloved. Since 1985 the Baffins Pond Association has been actively promoting and protecting the pond as a centre of community life. At a 'spring clean' of the pond in 2005, volunteers hauled items such as a shopping trolley, three bicycles, a TV and two teddy bears out of the pond! Bird watchers also actively lobby for the pond's protection.

The grand duchy takes its love of the pond one step further than other community groups. While it doesn't actually clean the pond or petition for the protection of fauna, it does obsessively make the 43,000-sq-metre pond area – and especially the three tiny islands in it – the centre of a whole new way of life.

LOCATION

The grand duchy is in Portsmouth, England. It exists on three *tiny* uninhabited islands in a small pond in a park on Tangier Rd, bordered by Neville Rd and Hayling Ave. The pond is accessible by footpath from each of these roads.

FACTS ABOUT THE LAGOAN ISLES

WEBSITE http://lagoan-isles-gov.tripod.com

FOUNDED 16 August 2005

HEAD OF STATE Grand Duke Louis (b Robert Harold Stephens, on 28 August 1985)

LANGUAGES English (official), Lagoan (regional)

AREA 43,000 sq metres

POPULATION Five

NATIONAL BIRD Swan

AERIAL VIEW OF THE LAGOAN ISLES AND SURROUNDING COUNTRY

NATIONAL TREE Willow tree (found on all of the Duchy's islands)

HISTORY

Baffins Farm records, complete with pond, date back to the year 1194. By the 18th century it was part of Portsmouth's grand Milton Manor. The pond that now houses the Grand Duchy of the Lagoan Isles was – by the 19th century – being used by local farmers. Early in the 20th century it became a park, available for use by Portsmouth residents. Coming under threat of destruction by property developers in 1938, the pond and surrounds were saved after a groundswell of local support.

As the 20th century progressed, interest in the health of the pond increased, resulting in numerous restorative and modernising programmes. The formation of the Baffins Pond Association in the mid-1980s further strengthened the pond's chances for a long and healthy future.

The pond at the centre of the Grand Duchy attracts members of the local community interested in a recreational reserve that can host both natural and man-made features. In addition to people, Baffins Pond is popular with Canada and barnacle geese, coot, moorhen, tufted duck, mallard and swan. According to John Bastable, a local birding authority, you might even see little grebe, cormorant and pochard wading in the water or setting webbed feet onto grand duchy land.

Visitors interested in observing and feeding the local birds are asked to only use grain – essential for the well-being of the birds and to maintain a healthy pond. Suitable feed can be purchased from shops along Tangier Rd. Fauna is further encouraged through the establishment and protection of suitable plant life. The local council conducts periodic dredging of the pond, designed to remove silt and man-made rubbish, and also conducts pond health programmes, establishing reed beds and oxygenating plant populations.

Small humans are made welcome in the surrounding parkland with provision of a large play area featuring a sand pit, while larger humans are attracted by regular community celebrations.

Any description of the recent history of the pond is incomplete without mentioning George Benham, a local hero who organised the first community-led efforts to reclaim the pond from neglect and vandalism. While George died in 2004, his legacy – a clean, healthy and well-loved natural asset – remains.

GRAND DUCHY TODAY

While the local community remains proud of the pond, one local resident wanted to elevate the pond's prominence well beyond its humble station. Discovering that while the pond was council land, the small islands in the pond are (apparently) not mentioned in any council documents, 19-year-old Robert Stephens (inspired by King Danny Wallace of Lovely and Prince Roy of Sealand) declared them a new, independent nation in 2005.

FESTIVALS & EVENTS

Along with traditional Western holidays, the Grand Duchy of the Lagoan Isles celebrates several unique holidays, including the following:

3 FEBRUARY: LAGOAN LAUGHING DAY

Lagoan citizens spend Laughing Day listening to the song 'I Love to Laugh' from the film *Mary Poppins*. As if once wasn't already once too many, the citizens play the song over and over and over and over…

27 JULY: NATIONAL HUGGING DAY

A day to simply hug, this national day is celebrated with a nation-wide hug-a-thon.

THE LAGOAN ISLES' NATIONAL ANTHEM

(to the tune of 'God Save the Queen')

God Save Our Islands Three
Give them reality
For all to see

Give us a bolder voice
And let us all rejoice
Lord, give us all a choice
To live in Peace

God Save Our Islands Three
Give them reality
For all to see

Grand Duke of Majesty
Nation because of thee
Family of Royalty
To live in Peace

God Save Our Islands Three
Give them reality
For all to see

One day we all will be
Dancing because we're free
Oh Lord we'll be with thee
To live in Peace

---

16 AUGUST: LAGOAN DAY!

The Grand Duchy's national Independence Day is accompanied by songs, flag-waving, parties and the occasional parade. Just like *your* national day, really.

28 AUGUST: GRAND DUKE'S BIRTHDAY

Marking Grand Duke Louis' birthday, this holiday is usually celebrated with a royal tea-party and birthday cake.

FACTS FOR THE VISITOR

CITIZENSHIP

Applications for citizenship are welcomed, and are assessed on a case-by-case basis. Contact the Lagoon Isles government for more information: lagoan-isles-gov@hotmail.co.uk. God knows how those who are rejected must feel.

EMBASSIES

The Lagoan Isles has rapidly established a global diplomatic presence that is the envy of many other, older, micronations. Nine recognised nations – including India, Ireland, the UK, Australia, China and the USA – house embassies (whether their governments know it or not). The Isles has also established 'Hand of Friendship' treaties with other micronations, including Molossia and Lovely.

THINGS TO SEE & DO

Aside from enjoying the peaceful ambience and delightful birdlife on the pond itself, there are several interesting attractions in the area.

PORTSMOUTH HISTORIC DOCKYARD

With an astonishing collection of historic ships, the **Portsmouth Dockyard** (☎ 023-9283 9766; Victory Gate, HM Naval Base Portsmouth, Hampshire) is one of the top 10 heritage attractions in the UK. With a protective wall built at the site in 1212 at the behest of King John, the dockyard became the world's first dry dock in 1495.

Henry VIII bestowed the official status of Naval Dockyard in 1540, and it has been the home of the British Royal Navy since then. As well as the **Royal Naval Museum**, the docklands also houses many of the most important seafaring vessels of British history. The main attraction is the HMS *Victory*, Admiral Lord Nelson's flagship at the 1805 Battle of Trafalgar. Tours are available.

BLUE REEF AQUARIUM
Situated in Southsea, adjoining Portsmouth and quite close to the grand duchy, the **aquarium** (☎ 023-9287 5222; Clarence Esplanade, Southsea; adult/child £6.95/4.50; ☼ 10am-5pm) displays the usual aquarium fare: sharks, seahorses, crabs, rays and clownfish. With an underwater tunnel, an otter enclosure and a warm-water display, the aquarium is very popular with kids. The aquarium has

been voted Visitor Attraction of the Year by Tourism South East.

SPINNAKER TOWER
This new **observation tower** (☎ 023-9285 7520; Gunwharf Quays, Portsmouth; adult/child £4.95/4; ☼ 10am-5pm, 10am-10pm Sat), shooting 170m into the sky, not only gives great views, it is an impressive piece of architectural design in its own right. England's south coast never looked so good – on a clear day, the view extends over 35km. And it'd be a crappy day indeed if you couldn't spot the Grand Duchy. With Europe's biggest glass floor, the tower challenges visitors to 'walk on air'.

Principality of Vikesland

Motto: Freedom, Equality and Strength

Although a newcomer to the micronational world, Vikesland's government has been working hard to establish a system of sustainable government, in the hope it might one day peacefully separate from Canada's rule. With a comprehensive constitution (including a chapter of fundamental rights and bills renouncing war), a royal council to oversee government, and outward-looking policies, the principality is well positioned to take its place at the forefront of micronational affairs.

Among the policies of the Vikesland government, a vow to never tax its citizens is foremost. Vikesland intends to fund the operations of the new nation almost entirely through online business enterprises. While it currently does not sell anything, plans are in place to establish a profitable postal service.

The name Vikesland honours the adventuring spirit of Vikings, while also highlighting the principality's physical land base.

LOCATION

Vikesland occupies two land areas in the province of Manitoba, Canada. The town of Brandon is about 210km due west of Winnipeg on TC-1 (Yellowhead Hwy). Royal Ranch is on the edge of Riding Mountain National Park, about 125km by road northeast of Brandon.

FACTS ABOUT VIKESLAND

WEBSITE www.vikeslandic.com

FOUNDED 1 July 2005

HEAD OF STATE His Royal Majesty, Prince Christopher I

LANGUAGE English

CURRENCY Vikeslandic Crown (pegged to the US dollar at a rate of one to one). The Royal Bank of Vikesland plans to produce bank notes and coins in the near future.

IN THE BLOOD

His Royal Majesty, Prince Christopher I, has always been interested in monarchies – particularly the tales of Arthurian legend and the conquests of Napoleon. This interest has been further spurred by the prince's own noble and revolutionary ancestry.

With a bloodline tracing back to French Seigneurs, the prince is also a blood relative of famed 19th-century Canadian figure Louis Riel. Regarded by many as a hero and others as a traitor, Riel fought on behalf of the Métis people, was instrumental in the establishment of the province of Manitoba, and even declared a provisional Canadian government for a brief period, in order to protect Canadian land from takeover by the US.

A period of exile in the USA and time spent in an asylum in Quebec was followed by a move to Saskatchewan, where Riel was hailed as the spiritual leader of the still-downtrodden Métis people. When a series of violent confrontations resulted in the killing of police officers and others by Métis and First Nations people, Louis Riel was deemed guilty by association. He was eventually hanged in 1855.

Vikesland's development owes much to the prince's ancestry. The prince himself acknowledges that it is in his blood 'to be independent, and to strive for greater things'.

AREA As citizens join the Vikesland family, they transfer their property to the new nation, so the total land area is constantly growing. The Royal Ranch claims 650,000 sq metres.

POPULATION 25

PEOPLE & CULTURE

Vikeslandic culture is similar to the cultures of neighbouring Canada and the nearby US. Vikeslanders are famously easy-going, peace-loving people who enjoy the out-doors, as well as indoor pursuits such as watching movies.

Citizenship is available. The most common form of citizenship – becoming a Cyber Citizen – affords applicants the right to vote and participate in the social life of Vikesland. To run for office or join the security forces, however, full citizenship is required. The Vikesland government does not issue passports at this time.

FESTIVALS & EVENTS

In addition to standard Western holidays such as Christmas, Vikesland also observes two unique celebrations in the year. **Second Halloween** (first Saturday of December) is celebrated by carving a pumpkin, watching scary films and eating junk food. Vikesland celebrates its founding during the four-day **Declaration Days celebration** (1–4 July).

FACTS FOR THE VISITOR

PLACES TO STAY

Victoria Inn (☎ 204-725 1532; 3550 Victoria Ave, W Brandon, Manitoba; r from CAD$95) Located in downtown Brandon, the Victoria Inn has well-appointed rooms that feature a DVD player, Internet access, refrigerator and coffee maker. The Inn has an indoor swimming pool and fitness centre available to guests, and serves a complimentary hot breakfast daily.

Royal Oak Inn & Suites (☎ 204-728 5775; 3130 Victoria Ave W Brandon, Manitoba; r from CAD$85) The 156-room Royal Oak Inn offers good rooms and good service to weary travellers.

THE PRINCE AND PRINCESS

VIKESLAND MEDIA EMPIRE

More than any other micronation, Vikesland has taken firm steps towards the establishment of a broadcasting network, designed to serve the micronational community by providing news, access and distribution. Prince Christopher I has invited all interested micronationalists to contribute audio and video to these broadcast channels.

While the planned online radio station, VBC Radio 1, has yet to capture the hearts and minds of the broader micronational community, Vikesland has also established a video channel, VBC1. The channel features videos such as *The Royal Ranchlands*, a montage documenting the bucolic lifestyle enjoyed by most Vikeslanders.

The prince is also focussing his professional skills on the production of a documentary on micronations. Having worked in the broadcast media industry for 13 years, the prince hopes to combine his observations as a micronational leader with his professional experience to explore the fascinating world of micronationalism.

Rooms come with the 'Guaranteed 110% Clean' policy, which promises to give guests a complete refund as well as a 10% discount on subsequent stays if the rooms are not found to be clean. During the winter, there is also a heated underground carpark, guaranteeing a speedy getaway when you leave.

PLACES TO EAT

Remington's Seafood & Steakhouse (☎ 204-571 3838; Town Centre, 800 Rosser Ave cnr 9th St, Brandon, Manitoba) Remington's is an upmarket steakhouse serving great meals with flair. With appetisers including nachos ($8) and popcorn shrimp ($9) and generous mains such as rack of lamb ($29) and blue crab and spinach stuffed chicken ($25), this is a place designed to keep the family happy and sated. There are a couple of simple vegetarian options. Look out for the impressive wine list, specialising in great midrange wines from California and Australia.

Double Happiness Restaurant (☎ 204-728 6388; 608 Rosser Ave, Brandon, Manitoba) While not exactly a gourmet Chinese dining experience, Double Happiness nevertheless serves great take-out–style Chinese fare at bargain prices. While the setting is humble, the food is dependable, with the buffet a great option for hungry travellers.

THINGS TO SEE & DO

Westman Reptile Gardens (☎ 204-763 4030; www .reptilegardens.ca; Thompson Rd; adult/under 16 $5/3; ⏰ 10am-8pm Mon-Sat, 12-5pm Sun) About 30km east of Brandon's town centre is Canada's largest reptile exhibit. Located near the Canadian Armed Forces' CFB Shilo base, Dave Shelvey's Reptile Gardens features a chameleon, snakes, turtles, alligators, lizards, iguanas and spiders. The highlight of the exhibit is the only two Nile crocodiles on display in Canada.

THE IMPOSING VIKESLAND VILLA

Art Gallery of Southwestern Manitoba (☎ 204-727 1036; www.agsm.ca; 710 Rosser Ave, 2nd fl; ☺ 10am-6pm Mon-Sat, to 9pm Thu) This nonprofit, free gallery, located in downtown Brandon next to the town centre, offers an ever-changing programme of exhibitions with an emphasis on contemporary Manitoban art. The attached **School of Art** offers workshops for all ages throughout the year.

GETTING THERE & AWAY

Visits to the principality, while not impossible, are generally unwanted. Because almost all Vikeslandic territory is privately owned by individual citizens, mass tourism and unrestricted access are not possible. The areas around the principality are beautiful, however, and will give travellers a sense of the treasured Vikeslandic lands.

Those wishing to appeal for special-circumstances visiting approval should apply via email to government@vikeslandic .com.

GREAT UNITED KISEEAN KINGDOM

The Great United Kiseean Kingdom (GUKK) was an unlikely micronation founded in 1992 in Romania and Finland. Unaware of other micronations, King John-Lucas I founded the Kiseean Kingdom while holidaying in Finland. Encouraged by his family, the young Romanian royal then set about establishing national administrative systems.

By 1996 the kingdom was already producing a regular *Free Kiseenia Gazette* and a magazine featuring works by the king's parents, who were both artists. A postal service was established and – the following year – the first stamps were issued.

About this time, the king became aware of other micronations, and set about establishing diplomatic relations. This contact led him to attempt to create an intermicronational postal service, advocating the establishment of an agreed value for stamps, and trade process for mail between micronations.

At its height, the kingdom comprised 10 geographical zones, of which three were occupied (two in Bucharest, Romania, and the third in Helsinki, Finland).

Sadly, the GUKK went into a self-imposed hiatus in September 2004, from which it has yet to emerge. In a micronational world crying out for shared systems, many patiently wait for the day when the Kiseean Kingdom emerges from the shadows to continue its mission of fostering cooperation between micronations.

Kingdom of Romkerhall

The Kingdom of Romkerhall looks like it was plucked straight from the minds of the Brothers Grimm – it's actually a 19th-century German hotel featuring all the monarchistic trimmings from that period, plus more glitter than Gary. In winter, when snow frosts the roof, fairytale fantasies are guaranteed. But will they be pleasant ones?

Inside the kingdom, glittering bedrooms and throne rooms complete the scene, even if they are completely over the top – talk about gilding the lily. Outside is an equally outrageous royal carriage, which newlyweds seem to love.

But Romkerhall is not simply a fancy gimmick to sell a hotel; like many good micronations, it's taken advantage of a loophole in the law to proclaim its own state of being and to secede from the macronation surrounding it.

LOCATION

By the Romke River in Germany's Okertal Valley, part of Lower Saxony's Upper Harz highland region.

FACTS ABOUT ROMKERHALL

WEBSITE www.koenigreich-romkerhall.de

FOUNDED 1988

HEAD OF STATE Queen Erina

LANGUAGES German and English

CURRENCY Okerthaler (legal tender within the hotel)

POPULATION Varies depending on hotel bookings

HISTORY

The actual hotel was originally a hunting lodge commissioned by King George V in the 19th century as part of his Hanover Kingdom. But when the German monarchy ended in 1918, the lodge and its surrounding area were forgotten about; when parishes were subsequently drawn up, the lodge was never officially assigned to any of them.

According to Romkerhall's Baron Lechner, when the parishes were redrawn in 1970 the lodge was again left out of the picture and Romkerhall was once more in no man's land – in essence a 'municipality free', independent territory. Some time after, the baron purchased the lodge after a fire went

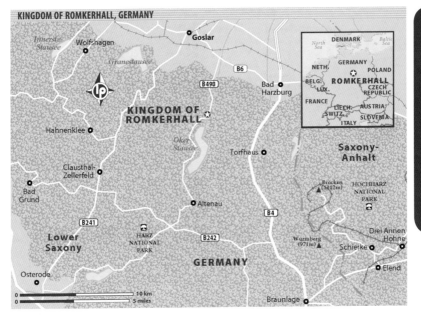

through it, but it took him a few years before he could decide upon a full plan of action.

First he set about renovating it in the completely over-the-top style you see today. Then he drew the attention of the Princess Erina von Sachsen, Duchess to Saxonia (who was married to the grandchild of Friedrich-August III, Saxony's last king). In 1988, while declaring the new state of Romkerhall – 'the world's smallest kingdom' – he invited the Duchess into his world, pronouncing her Queen of Romkerhall.

In 2003 the baron put his Kingdom up for sale on eBay: bids began at $37 million and later ballooned to $60 million. It's

THE ROYAL WHEELBARROW IN ALL ITS GLORY

unsure whether he was serious or not, and when Romkerhall was withdrawn from sale, it gave credence to the view that this was another example of the Baron's wacky sense of humour.

GEOGRAPHY & CLIMATE

Romkerhall is surrounded by slate-and-granite mountains. The Harz Mountains have their own temperate microclimate: summers are cool and winters feature heavy snow.

ECONOMY

It's a hotel – that's the economy. And Romkerhall is terribly well suited to wedding tourism. What bride and groom worth their confetti wouldn't love to sleep like kings and queens, ride in a royal carriage, and allow themselves to be pampered in Romkerhall's 'state restaurant' with a royal-sized feast? Loopy ones, actually.

Stamps (naturally) are produced and Romkerhall's coinage is highly sought after, so much so that fake 'Romkerhalls' have sprung up on the Internet pretending to sell the kingdom's currency for serious cash.

The baron also sells titles of nobility and this has got him into an ongoing battle with the German government. Because Romkerhall has such a long and verifiable history, the baron claims his titles are real German titles, but the government disputes this and seems to be quite annoyed by the assertion. The average person, however, could probably tell the baron's tongue is wedged at least part way in his cheek by some of the nomenclatures on offer – 'Royal Yard Supplier' and 'Royal Yard Photographer' among them.

GOVERNMENT

Queen Erina is the titular head of state, but the real power behind the throne is Baron Lechner, Romkerhall's owner.

PEOPLE & CULTURE

Considering the transient nature of the population, the culture is varied, to say the least.

FACTS FOR THE VISITOR

PLACES TO STAY & EAT

Romkerhall's Royal Restaurant is an ostentatious 70-person eating hall; specialties include baked chicken, duck and goose, plus sauerkraut and wine. The kingdom also offers 50 beds in 28 rooms with en suites (☎ 05 329 823; rooms per person from €25).

THINGS TO SEE & DO

The area surrounding Romkerhall is delightful and includes stretches of Saxonian forest and the popular **Romke Waterfall**. **Hiking** in the Harz Mountains is popular.

SUNGLASSES ARE ESSENTIAL WHEN VISITING ROMKERHALL

GETTING THERE & AWAY

If driving from the north, west, south or southeast of Germany, take the A7 highway to the Seesen exit – from there it's a 45-minute drive through the Harz region to Romkerhall. From the east or northeast, drive via Harzburg and Goslar to Oker – from there it's another 4km to the kingdom.

If travelling by train, alight at Gosslar, Harzburg or Altenau; from which there's a regional bus that takes a direct route to Romkerhall.

There are no visa requirements.

A COSY ROMKERHALL SUITE

IBROSIAN PROTECTORATE

The Ibrosian Protectorate is an umbrella government that looks after the affairs of several constituent members, located within the territorial boundary of Great Britain. The primary political state – the Great Commonwealth of the Ibrosian Democracy – has been operating alongside the government of the UK since 1999.

A complicated federal structure exists to define and rule this nation, which claims land 'about the size of a large field or two' scattered across several territories mostly in central Scotland. It has a chief of state – Lord Protector of the Commonwealth, the Duke of Amberly – a prime minister and a parliament consisting of two houses.

While the Ibrosians have their own currency – the Great Commonwealth Pound (GC£) – and many other traditional trappings of nationhood, they are also fairly isolationist. While citizens of the UK and Ireland are generally permitted entry, the Ibrosian Protectorate only shares diplomatic ties with one other micronation – the Realm of Strathclyde, which is based around (and lays claim to) Glasgow in Scotland.

Of particular note is Ibrosia's unique decimal approach to times and dates. A 24-hour day (or 'Dai' in the Ibrosian language) is divided into 10 'deciDais' of 144 minutes each. These are broken down further into centiDais (14.4 minutes), milliDais (1.44 minutes), microDais and even nanoDais.

The annual calendar, too, is decimalised, with 10 months, each containing 36 or 37 days. It's a perpetual calendar (every date falls on the same day each year), with an 'intercalary day' occurring between the fifth and sixth months every year.

Sovereign Kingdom of Kemetia

Comprising just 4047 sq metres of Royal Domain land, as well as a significantly smaller plot called the Province of Kemetia Minor, this fledgling nation shows all the signs of a long and fascinating future under the leadership of its tough-talking king. Though still young (King Adam was born in 1989, making him one of the youngest national leaders in the world), the sovereign has already shown an ability to deal proactively with national threats, ranging from attempted coups to the infamous attack on his motorcade while on a diplomatic trip to the USA (see Attack Near Lake Michigan, p100).

Kemetians are very proud of their independence and national identity, proclaiming that they do differ from the nation that surrounds them (England), particularly in their interest in the arts and classical music – the king himself is a composer.

LOCATION

The Sovereign Kingdom of Kemetia has been established just outside Petersfield, about 20 minutes north of Portsmouth in Hampshire, England.

FACTS ABOUT KEMETIA

WEBSITE www.kingdomofkemetiagov.tk

FOUNDED June 2005

HEAD OF STATE King Adam (Adam Raphael Isaacs Hemmings); Prime Minister Jolyon Lloyd-Davies

CAPITAL Stonerdale City

LANGUAGES English (official), with minorities also speaking Hebrew, Sinhalese, Welsh and French

CURRENCY Debens (Db)

AREA 160,000 sq metres

POPULATION 112

TIME GMT/UTC 0 (Kemetian Summer Time during daylight savings)

HISTORY

Kemetia formed in 2005 when Adam Isaacs Hemmings and an 'entourage of loyal supporters' claimed territory in the English county of Hampshire for the Sovereign Kingdom of Kemetia. The nation started life as an absolute monarchy, but soon yielded to the people and transformed into a constitutional monarchy.

TOUGH TALK

The seemingly endless drama that has surrounded King Adam since the formation of the Sovereign Kingdom of Kemetia has provoked some extraordinary oratory outbursts. None has been more angry or more powerful that this speech, disseminated as an audio file on the day of Kemetia's attack by previously friendly neighbouring nations. This is an edited extract of the king's speech:

Today, September 8th, 2005: a date that will live in infamy. The Sovereign Kingdom of Kemetia was suddenly and deliberately attacked by the twin kingdoms of xxxx and xxxx. The Kingdom of Kemetia was at peace with that nation and, at the soliciting of the twin kingdoms, was still in conversation with its government and its kings. It will be recorded that… this attack was deliberately planned for many days, or even weeks. During the intervening time, the twin kingdoms' government has deliberately sought to deceive Kemetia with false statements and the expression of hope for a continued peace.

The facts of today speak for themselves. As commander-in-chief of the army and navy, I have directed that all measures be taken for our defence. However, always will our nation remember the character of this onslaught against us. No matter how long it may take us to overcome this premeditated invasion, the Kemetian people, in their righteous might, will win through to absolute victory.

Hostilities exist! There is no blinking at the fact that our people, our territory and our interests are in grave danger. With the unbending determination of our people, we will gain the inevitable triumph, so help us God!

KING ADAM SHAKES HANDS WITH MINISTER OF SECURITY SAMUEL SIMPSON-CREW

While the details are closely guarded by the inner sanctum of Kemetia, only eight days after the declaration of sovereignty, a coup was staged in Kemetia. An unnamed member of the inaugural Kemetian government apparently seized power and ruled for 14 days. Few additional details are known. In a statement following this incident, King Adam announced simply that 'the revolt was completely crushed and order has returned'.

Trouble seems to follow the king. Or perhaps he courts it. On his first diplomatic mission outside of Europe, an event occurred that sent shockwaves through the micronational community. While travelling in Chicago, USA, in late October 2005, the king was attacked while his motorcade was moving

KING ADAM

Michigan, USA. Analysts wonder whether this nonspecific threat constitutes a form of 'payback' for the apparent assassination attempt in the nearby state if Illinois.

According to King Adam, Kemetia has a standing army of 40 men and women.

ECONOMY

Kemetia is principally a primary resources economy. The land around the capital is comprised mainly of sandy, acidic soil, although the soil in other Kemetian regions varies greatly, with tracts of chalk and clay land. This variety means that a wide range of crops can be grown on Kemetian soil; at present these crops are consumed internally, but the ministry of agriculture and the ministry of foreign affairs are currently investigating the possibility of exporting soft fruit as a source of foreign currency.

The ministry of defence owns its own tracts of land on which to grow food for the 40-person military and the mysterious General Intelligence Department.

peacefully through the streets. The king's security forces quelled any threat and the visit proceeded without further incident.

It appears that in Kemetia's short existence, it has raised the ire of sinister forces that seem committed to destabilising the nation. The king has encountered trouble with people impersonating him. He has offered a reward of £3 and a seat in the parliament for anyone who offers information leading to the capture of these troublemakers…

According to official reports, Kemetia is assessing land-grab opportunities in Ecuador, Belize, the Philippines and Polynesia. While the macronational community would shudder at the inevitably violent implications of such a move, the king has also proclaimed his plans to invade an unidentified island somewhere in northern

PEOPLE & CULTURE

While Kemetia is officially a secular nation, freedom of religious expression is afforded the citizenry. The majority of the population are secular or Church of England, with Jewish (the Royal Family), Catholic, Buddhist, and many other minorities present.

All applicants are freely granted Kemetian citizenship.

ATTACK NEAR LAKE MICHIGAN

The following is the official regal press release following the stunning attack on the king of Kemetia while he was on a diplomatic visit to Illinois, USA:

Today, October 27th 2005, the king's motorcade was rammed and attacked by a lone attacker in a white car in Chicago, USA. No injuries are reported to have happened to the king or his family. After thorough investigation, the series of events were as follows: after being given a tour of the city, the royal motorcade stopped at a stop sign on the street facing Lake Michigan and were to proceed to an exhibition at the Museum of Science and Industry. Once the motorcade had turned and was travelling down the street, a white car attempted to cut in front of the car the king was travelling in. As a result the king's car hit the car of the attacker disabling it and the suspected detonation device that may have been used to detonate the motorcade. All was wrapped up nicely by the accompanying Retinue and the local police who were soon despatched to the scene. All are well and have returned to the Hillcrest Royal Palace and Courtyard Guest Palace.

THINGS TO SEE & DO

During autumn and winter (September to January), the atmosphere in Kemetia changes as the weather closes in and restricts the activities of the citizenry. While Kemetians rarely venture from their fireside, there is one event that keeps Kemetian blood pumping.

The **Grand Prince Ken Walk** is a major state sponsored event in which participants walk from the Royal Palace to the town of Priors Dean. This walk is to commemorate Grand Prince Ken – an important figure in Kemetia's development – and his energetic spirit. After the walk, a reception is held with participants imbibing the renowned Hemmings Whisky and Prince John's Brew, served with gherkins and perhaps a side of Kemetian smoked salmon.

According to the king, any visitor during this period will end up mimicking this routine: 'spending great tracts of time reading and talking in the warm households occupied by the population, doing nothing more physically gruelling than roasting chestnuts or watching a firework display; Kemetia's pyrotechnics industry being a cornerstone of the economy, and of any celebration'.

TALOSSA – GONE BUT NOT FORGOTTEN

The glorious Kingdom of Talossa – inspiration for many micronations throughout the 1980s, '90s and beyond – was founded in the bedroom of a 13-year-old on 26 December 1979. Robert Ben Madison took the throne of his new kingdom, and ruled alone for more than a year. In 1981 he began admitting citizens, and the Kingdom of Talossa was on its way to glory...and ultimate oblivion.

King Robert I, having extended his territorial claim to include a large part of the city of Milwaukee, Wisconsin, opened up the political process to Talossan citizens, declaring a constitutional monarchy in 1985. The following year saw a crisis in which Robert was deposed, although he was restored to the throne in 1988.

With well-developed, good-natured governmental systems (the national cuisine was Taco Bell) and an active approach to intermicronational affairs, Talossa was – for two decades – one of the great micronational superpowers. With such open policies and an outward-looking philosophy, though, all of the worst excesses of the global micronational movement emerged. King Robert closed his kingdom down in late 2005.

While there are still online groups claiming to be Talossa, Madison says that none of the original Talossan figures are involved. Citing the old adage 'local politics is so vicious because the stakes are so low', Madison says he had to withdraw from his creation because of constant political infighting. Isn't micronationalism mostly about fun? Madison says sadly, 'Part of the problem is that different people define "fun" in different ways'.

Aerican Empire

When Eric Lis created the Aerican Empire (pronounced *ah-erican*, like 'American' without the 'm'), he was the youngest micronational leader in history. At only five years old, this Montreal youngster already knew that a special future was ahead of him. The city-state he created has become one of the most visible nations in the micronational world, and has expanded to include several tracts of land around the world (not to mention a few, apparently, off-world as well).

Founded on a notion of complete silliness, the empire is active but – at the same time – quite secretive about its internal operations. While it has signed many treaties with other micronations, its leader, Eric, remains a shadowy figure, rarely seen by those in the outside world.

LOCATION

The Aerican Empire's main claim is 2.3 sq metres at its global headquarters and Canadian embassy in Montreal. Aside from several extraterrestrial claims, the Aerican Empire also claims a cow pasture 'somewhere', one square foot of land that changes location constantly, and – oddly – a large portion of suburban Melbourne, Australia, including the suburbs of Dandenong, Springvale and Chelsea, which it calls Psyche.

FACTS ABOUT THE AERICAN EMPIRE

WEBSITE www.aericanempire.com

FOUNDED May 1987

HEAD OF STATE Emperor Eric Lis

LANGUAGES English and Aerican (As befits a micronation, the Aerican language is described as a micro-language. It's a living, growing language, made up of words used in conjunction with English.)

AREA 2.3 sq metres

POPULATION Precise figures are unavailable, but it is believed that Aerica has just over 200 citizens

HISTORY

Forming a new nation is a rather serious undertaking, and it can be argued that – at five years old – Eric Lis was not fully equipped to cope with the birthpains of a nation. And so the first decade of the empire was a time of turbulence, with Aerican forces required to defend themselves against multiple attacks. Many of these attacks were from unknown forces; there are controversial murmurings that some of these attacks might actually have been the imaginings of a young boy.

Thankfully, though, divine salvation also revealed itself to Aericans in the form of the Great Penguin, a deity discovered in 1991, and described as a 'non-corporeal being' subservient to a greater god (see Religion, below). The Great Penguin has intervened to save the empire on occasion (most notably in 1998, when it apparently dropped a tree on the leader of mysterious invading forces).

The history of the empire from the late 1990s reads like a who's who of the micro-national world. Aerica – always with a smiling face to the world – formed treaties and alliances with many micronations (both real ones and those existing only online) in 1998 and 1999, including Federation Ark, Baja Arizona, Monastico and the Purple Bunny Federation.

GOVERNMENT

The empire is governed by a senate (each colony elects up to two senators) with a president elected from this body. The current president is Randy Walker, who won another four-year term at the beginning of 2006. There is also an inner council, made up of the emperor and a hand-chosen group of advisors.

PEOPLE & CULTURE

RELIGION

The official faith is Silinism, best described as a disorganised religion. Forsteri, the Great Penguin, looks over all Aericans. According to official sources, 'The Great Penguin is either a cosmic manifestation of an abstract principle or an abstract representation of a cosmic principle, depending on who you ask.'

NQTA

Aericans believe in the coming of Not-Quite-The-Apocalypse, heralded by the four 'Incompetent Riders', comprising a penguin, a platypus, a giant walnut and a fourth rider that can't quite be identified. Sure signs that the NQTA is upon us will include strange things happening, other strange things happening, really strange things happening, and it not quite being the Apocalypse.

LAWS

Aerica adheres to a general set of international laws and upholds the Geneva Convention. In addition, it has passed several specific laws, including the Murphy Law (which protects the empire if everything goes wrong) and the Hillary Clinton Act, which allows people to run for office in a location other than the one they're from.

Aericans are protected by members of Omega, the nation's imperial guard. These troops are equipped to deal with 'data transfer, hacking, spying, and other tasks of necessity'.

CITIZENSHIP & RESIDENCY

Citizenship is freely available, with most people taking advantage of the online application form. Residency is also possible, particularly if you happen to live in an area claimed by the empire.

FESTIVALS & EVENTS

Aerica celebrates many holidays. Here is a list of the more interesting of them:

Procrastinator's Day (2 Jan), to recover from New Year's **Emperor Norton Day** (8 Jan), the

SHROUDED IN MYSTERY, AERICAN FOUNDER AND EMPEROR, ERIC LIS

anniversary of the death of Emperor Joshua Norton I of the US (see p69); **Oops Day** (27 Feb), commemorating the day the Tower of Pisa became the Leaning Tower of Pisa; **Significant Historical Events Day** (28 Aug), commemorating important events that do not have their own day.

GETTING THERE & AWAY

Pierre Elliott Trudeau International Airport (PET), also known as Montréal Trudeau Airport, is about 21km west of downtown and is the centre of domestic, US and overseas flights. It is also the nearest airport to the Aerican Empire. The airport has good connections to the city by car, bus or metro (subway). The Québécois Bus Company runs Aérobus shuttles from PET Airport to downtown. At Station Aérobus, a smaller shuttle will pick you up and drop you anywhere in central downtown, free of charge. Driving to downtown Montreal from PET Airport will take roughly 20 to 30 minutes, although rush hour can extend your travelling time.

CASCADIA: FOR HUMANS, HUMANOIDS & HOMINIDS ALIKE

Over the years various secessionist movements have laid claim to North America's northwest coastal region: the Canadian state of British Columbia and the US states of Washington and Oregon (with territorial variations according to the movement). The idea supposedly dates back to 1803, when US President Thomas Jefferson came up with the idea of an independent nation – the Republic of the Pacific. Later secessionists proposed a 'State of Jefferson', expanding upon the original notion that the Oregonian and Californian borders were arbitrarily drawn and cut across the unique demographics of the region.

In some quarters this whole business is taken very seriously indeed. Some movements have threatened armed resistance to unite the region, while others have drawn upon the futurist ideas of author Ernest Callenbach, who described a new country, 'Ecotopia', in his 1975 novel of that name, formed from the seceded states of Washington and Oregon along with Northern California.

Callenbach's fictional country was founded on the development of sophisticated sustainable-development technologies and alternative social systems, including mag-lev public transport, 20-hour working weeks, collective ownership of businesses and farms, elimination of pollution, worship of trees and plant life, women in political power and ritualistic war games. The whole idea has been described as 'the perfect balance between humans and the environment'.

In reality, there's a real-world 'bioregion' that cuts across the northwest coastal region, a highly distinct geographical area with geographic boundaries determined by the natural world: plant life, soils and so on. In recent decades, secessionists have taken to calling the area 'Cascadia' and a lot of their rhetoric describes secession along Callenbachian lines. As one activist reports, 'Cascadians' possess a 'deep psychological identification with their dwelling place', a state of mind that derives from their very close identification with the Earth. So the argument goes, this identification manifests itself in a set of Cascadian cultural and societal mores – including philosophical beliefs and linguistic characteristics – that are endemic to the region and utterly divorced from the rest of the continent.

All of this can be heavy going indeed, unless your name is Lyle Zapato, the founder of the satirical Republic of Cascadia movement. The republic's 'official website' displays a warped sense of humour that embraces '50s paranoid technologies such as mind control and alien invasion, making it hard to know whether Zapato is mocking the high-minded ideals of 'real' Cascadians or the oddball nature of micronational and secessionist movements in general.

The website details the existence of a Cascadian Sasquatch Militia, a cadre of Big Foot warriors ready to repel invasion by howling very loudly or, failing that, 'de-limbing' the enemy. And it claims that Cascadia 'has not yet achieved sheep-cloning technology [but] it is close – watch out Scotland!' The site also contains this admonishment: 'The Republic of Cascadia is not yet officially recognised by Canada, the United States of America, or the United Nations. Not that it is any of their business'.

In an exceedingly strange fashion, Zapato's Cascadian parodies paint a charming picture of a territory that is quite apart from the rest of the continent, even if it's really just a 'state of mind' more than a state of physical coordinates.

LYLE ZAPATO'S VERSION OF THE CASCADIAN FLAG

FURTHER READING
- **Republic of Cascadia** (http://zapatopi .net/cascadia) Lyle Zapato's site.
- **Republic of Cascadia** (http://republic-of -cascadia.tripod.com) A more serious version of Cascadian independence, with articles on Callenbachian ideals.

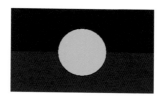

Principality of Trumania

(aka Republic of Trumania; Trumanist Republic of Trumania)

Motto: *Ullam-aime* (Ever Ready)

Sitting in the chilly waters of Puget Sound, not far south of Seattle in the Pacific Northwest, Vashon Island is a semi-rural getaway popular with families, cyclists and lovers of the great outdoors. It is also home to the Republic (or principality, depending on who you believe) of Trumania, a nation comprising three districts and one autonomous region.

Inspired by the climactic scene in the 1998 film *The Truman Show*, in which the main character declares his world 'Trumania of the Burbank Galaxy', this insular little micronation has been established on private property. While it's highly unlikely that Trumania will lift its veil of secrecy and allow travellers to visit, its surrounds on Vashon Island – with a population of just 10,000 – make a nice stop-over.

LOCATION

Trumania is located in several small enclaves on Vashon Island in Puget Sound, Washington State, USA.

FACTS ABOUT TRUMANIA

WEBSITE www.trumania.cjb.net

FOUNDED 2004

GOVERNMENT Constitutional monarchy

HEAD OF STATE HRH Prince Joseph I (b 23 Feb 1990)

HEAD OF GOVERNMENT First Minister Dan Purkiss (b 25 Mar 1988)

CAPITAL Marylewood (population: eight)

LANGUAGE English

AREA 170,000 sq metres

POPULATION 27

DEFENCE Budget $300

ACTIVE TROOPS None

GEOGRAPHY

The Principality of Trumania is divided into three districts – Marylewood, Wellshore and Burnsley – each with a distinct character of its own, although only Marylewood is populated. There is also a single autonomous region called Holtshire which is governed by Trumania from a distance.

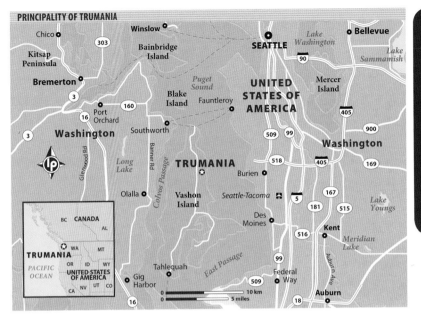

VASHON'S INDEPENDENT STREAK

Trumania is not the only example of the independent mindset of Vashon Island inhabitants. Eileen Wolcott, manager and co-owner of the Vashon Theatre – the only cinema on the island – happily went head-to-head with one of the world's biggest movie studios. Wolcott decided to cut short the run of a Harry Potter movie in favour of a prior agreement to host the musical stylings of the sizzling Bacon Brothers (featuring guitarist and part-time actor Kevin Bacon). This posed a dilemma for the massive Hollywood studio, which was behind one of Mr Bacon's great performances in *Mystic River*. Warners apparently expressed their unhappiness with the cancellation, but for Wolcott, a deal is a deal.

CITIZENSHIP & RESIDENCY

Citizenship is open, free and encouraged by the Trumanian government. A form available on the government website needs to be completed and submitted for processing. No statistics are given concerning citizenship numbers. Residency is not available.

GETTING THERE & AWAY

While this private nation is not open to foreigners, a trip to Vashon Island still makes a pleasant weekend break for visitors to the US Pacific Northwest.

Driving south from Seattle, follow the WA-99 for a couple of minutes and then veer right onto the West Seattle Bridge. Follow the road (it changes names to Fauntleroy Way) for about 8km to Lincoln Park. Take the Washington State Ferry service to Vashon. Ferries usually depart a couple of times each hour, with the trip taking about 15 minutes. A car on the ferry will cost US$13.60. Passengers alone are US$4.

The ferry arrives on the north coast of Vashon. From here, it's only about 10 or 15 minutes south to Trumania.

KINGDOM OF REDONDA: THEY CAN WRITE BUT THEY CAN'T RULE

In the late 1800s, mariner and entrepreneur Matthew Dowdy Shiell landed on the uninhabited Caribbean island of Redonda and declared it to be his personal kingdom, claiming that Queen Victoria had granted him the title of king on the condition that Redonda did not revolt against England. Shortly after, the British annexed the island for its phosphate resources and that certainly put paid to any ideas of independence.

Kingly accession, however, was another matter. In the 1940s, Shiell's son, Matthew Phipps Shiel (he dropped the second 'l' from his surname before styling himself King Felipe I), sold the title to John Gawsworth (King Juan I). Then Gawsworth offloaded the title, and that's where it all went haywire. No-one seems to know who owns it now and it's beyond the scope of this book to explore further, except to say that at one stage there were as many as six Men Who Would Be King. Today there are only three claimants of any real note, and all of them – in true micronational fashion – seem to be having a laugh at stuffy real-world attitudes more than anything else.

KING ROBERT THE BALD

Meet claimant No 1: King Robert the Bald, who lives in Antigua, and whose 'official' history of Redonda states that '[during] King Juan's stormy rule... royal sozzlement set in and he started hurling knighthoods around like confetti'.

Claimant No 2, King Leo, in turn writes: 'The impostor King Robert the Bald has had the gross impertinence to set his "claim" on the Internet, thereby...gratuitously insulting the present king from a distance of 3000 miles. Mon Dieu! Quelle situation! Do have a look! PS: Bob can be insulted via his email address: bob@xxxxx.xx'.

And finally, claimant No 3, Spanish author and academic Javier Marías (King Javier I), bestows 'royal Redondan titles' on various celebrities.

But even if we can't agree on who's king, let's at least agree that Redonda is undoubtedly the most literary entity in micronational history. During his day, Matthew Phipps Shiel was a significant (if erratic) novelist of fantasy and science fiction; John Gawsworth was a respected (if drunken) poet of 'neo-Georgian verse'; Javier Marías operates a Kingdom of Redonda publishing house; and both Javier and Robert have established literary prizes in the kingdom's name. King Robert claims to have written eight books, describing his latest collection of short stories as '[mostly] nonsense so it's a very light read'.

KING LEO

FURTHER READING
- **www.redonda.org** The website of King Leo's Redondan Foundation.
- **www.antiguanice.com/redonda** King Robert the Bald's website.
- **www.javiermarias.es/REDONDIANA/reinode redonda.html** Reino de Redonda, Javier Marías' site.

Part III

Grand Dreams

Independence can bear a heavy price, but sometimes realising a dream is worth the trouble. The nations in this section have all taken on challenges bigger than most of us would face in our lives.

Some have embarked on a public declaration of independence under the ever-watchful eye of a recognised nation. But challenges come bigger than just taking on one country's government: we also meet a nation that is taking on the entire global community of recognised nations, and is charting an uncertain future on the most desolate continent on earth. The weapons these daring micronations use include humour, good-will, art, resentment and history.

Brave? Stupid? Perhaps there's a bit of both in these fabulous examples of taking a stand and making dreams come true(ish).

Westarctica

Westarctica is the most active of the several micronations claiming land on the Antarctic continent. Established by an American citizen who traces his ancestry to the High Kings of Ireland, Westarctica is moving steadily to establish a frozen foothold in the large unclaimed portion of the frozen continent.

Westarctica's heads of state – initially Grand Duke Travis and, more recently, Grand Duke Philip – are active participants in micronational affairs. The nation has formed several alliances and was the recipient of five Norton Awards for Micronational Excellence and Achievement in 2005. It professes an ambition to actually inhabit the land it's claimed, and then open it up to tourism. Better pack the long johns.

LOCATION

Western Antarctica – also known as Marie Byrd Land – is the large portion of the Antarctic continent located directly below the South Pacific Ocean.

FACTS ABOUT WESTARCTICA

WEBSITE www.westarctica.com

FOUNDED 2001

GOVERNMENT Monarchy

HEAD OF STATE His Serene Majesty, Grand Duke Philip

STAMP FEATURING THE FORMER GRAND DUKE'S WEDDING

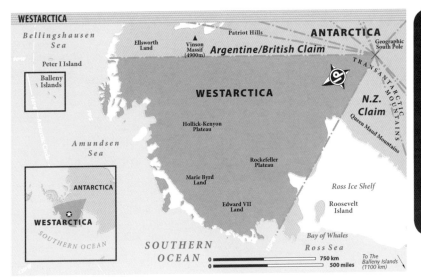

CAPITAL Peter I Island (disputed)

LANGUAGES English 85% (official), Spanish 10%, Norwegian 5%

ETHNIC GROUPS American 75%, Spanish 13%, English 6%, Norwegian 6%

RELIGIONS Christian 92% (Protestant 82%, Catholic 18%), other 8%

HISTORY

When Grand Duke Travis discovered that Marie Byrd Land (or Western Antarctica) was the only land in the world not claimed by any nation, it set an idea in motion. The Antarctic Treaty precludes nations from making a claim on this land, but – in an apparent loophole – says nothing about claims by individuals.

On 2 November 2001, Travis enacted his own little loophole, claiming the land as an individual and then founding a new nation in Marie Byrd Land. He named his new nation the Achaean Territory of Antarctica with the dispatch of a letter-of-claim to the Antarctica administration offices of Russia, France, Norway, Australia, New Zealand, Argentina, Chile, the US and the UK (see p112).

Over the next couple of years, the structures and operations of the nation were implemented and improved. Dukedoms were established and a Royal Charter was promulgated; no protests were received from any other nation throughout this time.

Following a 'religious experience' in June 2004, the Chancellery of the Achaean Territory was dissolved by Travis and the interim government of the Grand Duchy of Westarctica was declared. Travis anointed himself Grand Duke, designed a new flag, confessed his sins and declared Westarctica a Christian nation. Between July and October, all old titles were abolished and new members were appointed to the nobility.

THE THING AT BYRD STATION

In 1957 the US government established a scientific research station in Marie Byrd Land. Known as Byrd Station, the base was the largest in Western Antarctica and – in 1968 – became the site of the first drilling to penetrate through the Antarctic ice sheet (a depth of more than 3km).

There can be fewer less hospitable places on earth; stories and images from the station (and also McMurdo base) provided much of the inspiration for John Carpenter's classic schlock horror film *The Thing* (1982).

While Byrd Station ceased operations in 1972, a summer facility called Byrd Surface Camp was opened by the US Antarctic Program just a short distance east of the station.

At this time, rather than being entirely distracted by internal affairs of state, Grand Duke Travis issued a stern *démarche* to the Sudanese government (via Sudan's ambassador to the USA), decrying the government-sponsored brutality taking place in the Darfur region. In November 2004, Westarctica continued to look outward, bestowing the Noble Order of Westarctica on 11 reigning monarchs, and requesting formal diplomatic rela-

CLAIMING A COUNTRY

To Whom It May Concern,

I have been heavily studying the continent of Antarctica, and I have come to several conclusions. There are very few places on Earth where a man can truly be alone. Antarctica is one of those places. Its vast ice fields hold more than just frozen water, the entire continent holds the potential to unlock the secrets of our past.

Therefore, at this time, I deem it necessary to formally claim for myself all land between 90 degrees west and 150 degrees west and south of 60 degrees south to include all seas and ice shelves. This area will henceforth be known as 'The Achaean Territory of Antarctica'. The purpose of this acquisition is to secure the territory for research and development and promote future colonisation. Also, to protect it from those parties that would exploit the territory with misdeeds.

My intentions beyond that are my own.

Currently there are research stations and civilian scientists working within the borders of the Achaean Territory. These parties are now under my jurisdiction, and I am allowing them a four-year term to complete their research before insisting that they register their presence with my office. The physical capital of Achaea is located at 80 deg. 01 min. S, 119 deg. 31 min. W and has been named Achilles. I have every desire to become an active participant in the international future of Antarctica, including the placement of self-sponsored research stations and attendance at the International Antarctica Convention.

Respectfully,

His Eminence,
The Consul-General

tions with Taiwan, Latvia and the Sovereign Military Order of Malta.

It was perhaps because no reply was immediately forthcoming from these gestures of goodwill that Westarctica developed a more hawkish approach to international affairs in 2005. In February of that year, New Zealand's Balleny Islands (part of the Ross Dependency) were annexed by Westarctica. Only a month later, a note of thanks was received from the Grand Duke of Luxembourg, following a sympathy note sent by the Grand Duke. The deed was done, however, and despite granting the Balleny Islands some autonomy in May 2005, they remain disputed to this day.

Also in dispute is the region designated by Westarctica as the site of its future seat of government, Peter I Island. Norway claims this land, in apparent contravention of the Antarctic Treaty. According to official Westarctican sources, the two governments are in bilateral discussions to resolve this dispute. Westarctica is petitioning for the region to be designated a shared special administrative region.

The Bank of Westarctica was established in 2005 and the first postage stamp was issued. As with many micronations, sale of these items provides an important revenue stream to Westarctica. On 17 May 2005, a treaty of mutual recognition, cooperation, and friendship was signed with the Republic of Molossia at a meeting of the leaders of the two micronations in Washington DC. Former Grand Duke Travis is a graduate of the Molossian Military Academy.

In early 2006, Grand Duke Travis shocked Westarcticans and the global micronational population by abdicating. The duke cited family reasons, and a desire to pay more

HOME SWEET HOME

PRESIDENT BAUGH OF MOLOSSIA (R) WITH FORMER
GRAND DUKE TRAVIS

WESTARCTICA'S NATIONAL ANTHEM

'God Save Westarctica' (to the tune of 'God Save the Queen')

God save our grandest Duke
Give him the power to
Be just and strong
God save his majesty
Clothe him in piety
Cause everyone to see
The Grand Duke live long!
God save Westarctica
Flora and fauna
God save our land!
O Lord descend to us
Bless us with righteousness
Lay upon all of us
Your glorious hand

attention to his role as the Baron of Dunluce, as a direct descendant and heir to the Dunluce Barony in Antrim, Ireland. It seems that mild gulfstream breezes were a greater lure than the icy gales of Antarctica.

Travis handed power to the former Marquis de Merovingi and minister of in-formation, now Grand Duke Philip I. Key Westarctican policies remained unchanged after the handover, although the new Grand Duke indicated a desire to establish a ministry of the arts and a Westarctican news agency.

BOROVNIA

Two teenaged girls, Pauline Parker and Juliet Hulme, invented the nation of Borovnia in New Zealand in the 1950s. As events in their make-believe world intensified, their respective parents became increasingly alarmed, eventually forbidding the girls from seeing each other. In a fantasy-fuelled act of revenge, the girls killed Parker's mother.

The subsequent murder trial shocked quiet, conservative New Zealand, gave filmmaker Peter Jackson a perfect outlet for his visionary/horror talents (his wonderful 1994 film *Heavenly Creatures* is based on the true story), and gave fantasy micronations a bad reputation!

STAMPS ARE COOL

To issue a stamp is a long-standing, if slightly faded, means of asserting one's existence. For Cuban revolutionaries in the 1860s it was a technologically hip thing to do, French anti-republican royalists in the 1870s thought it a neat way to spread their ideas, and Julio Popper, a Romanian gold miner, printed one in January 1891 to make known he held the rights to mine gold in the Argentine half of Tierra del Fuego.

In a country with a population of one, messages written on the back of the hand reach their destination instantaneously. Nevertheless, burgeoning micronations are only too eager to align themselves with the institutional practices of more established states – printing pictures of lighthouses and movie stars, dogs and orchids onto sheets of adhesive paper, perforating them into detachable units to be sold to willing collectors as 'stamps'. The postmasters general of many a micronation need not worry that their stamps have to cover the cost of receiving and sorting and delivering mail. They've been issued solely with the tourist and the collector in mind. And at a face value at least a thousand times their cost of production, stamps appear to be a great source of income.

Every country worth its salt has a post office, even if it's an online souvenir shop. Some micronations do make the effort to offer a local service. A postcard sent from Hutt River Province's Nain post office to anywhere other than Hutt River Province's Nain post office needs its postage to be paid for twice, once for transport to Northampton and a stamp from Australia to pay for the rest of the journey. Hutt River Province is one of the most prodigious of stamp-issuing micronations, thanks to the efforts of former Prince Regent Kevin Gale (p24), who milked stamp collectors in the 1980s for all they were worth (and, according to the stamp-collecting emperor of Atlantium, pocketed the proceeds). He understood that stamps are an excellent source of revenue.

Or at least they used to be. In the good old days (the 19th century), men the likes of Charles-Marie David de Mayréna could be received in Paris as ruler of Sedang, a kingdom in Annam (Vietnam), charge expenses on credit from his nation's treasury, and order the printing of stamps. When de Mayréna shot through, the printer was left with the tab. Not to be the butt of a canard, the printers flooded the market, and the stamps sold very well until it was realised Sedang didn't exist.

Nowadays supply has just about killed off demand. Despite the best efforts of marketing campaigns such as Belgium's 'Stamps Are Cool', stamp collecting is a nostalgic hobby enjoyed by fewer and fewer retirees. Those who do collect can only do so selectively, hence the predominance of thematics – royalty, stamps on stamps, cats. Perhaps in response to this glut, collectors have moved away from traditional philately into the less-catalogued realm of 'cinderellas': the works of forgers and hoaxes, charities and micronations. The more popular cinderellas had a genuine use – an annual fundraising issue for the children's holiday camp on Elleore (p42), or a one shilling egg stabilisation charge from Western Australia – and are likely to be more valuable than a set of Hutt River Province stamps, which might be worth 10 cents. For the micronation, issuing stamps may be a symbolic political act, but it is quite likely to be a commercial flop.

However, post offices around the world, both real and micronational, continue to pump out product. Even new issues

for Sedang can be bought online, which are the fantasies of a 'Bruce Henderson' (or Grenville), a micronation stamp designer, who also creates stamps for a variety of invented countries with philatelic-themed names. His Raoul, for example, is named in honour of Raoul Charles de Thuin, an inveterate stamp forger. De Thuin was so prolific his plates and stock were bought in the 1960s by an American philatelic society for a vast sum on condition he never worked again – he moved to Ecuador and continued to sell his wares.

Unique stamps issued by imaginary countries are the staple of stamp painters, a movement that gathered steam in the early '70s and faded in the mid-'80s, and was documented and revived online in the late '90s. The myriad countries in the world of Donald Evans – Amis et Amants, Doland, Frandia, Yteke – are well worth the visit. Evans, an American who worked mainly in Holland, created albums of to-scale watercolour stamps depicting zeppelins and island scenes. Stamps used to be a popular form of daydreaming, Donald Evans' art encourages a similar, imaginary travel.

Maritime Republic of Eastport

Motto: We Like It This Way

To most citizens of the US, Annapolis, on Chesapeake Bay in Maryland, is known for the great US Naval Academy located there. So it's perhaps surprising that, just a short stroll from the place where America trains its navy and marine forces, a civil protest in the closing years of last century led to the emergence of a flourishing nation.

Head southeast from the Maryland State House in central Annapolis, and you'll soon hit the ironically named Compromise St. After a minute, you'll arrive at a bridge. Or, rather, *the* bridge. On the north side, it's Annapolis. On the south, it's Eastport. And it's more than just Spa Creek separating them.

LOCATION

The Maritime Republic of Eastport is located on the western shore of Chesapeake Bay, surrounded by the state of Maryland in the northeastern USA.

FACTS ABOUT EASTPORT

WEBSITE www.themre.org

FOUNDED 1998

HEAD OF STATE Premier Jessica Pachler – 2006 (the premier is elected annually)

HISTORY

In 1998 the drawbridge across Spa Creek was scheduled for repair by the Maryland State Highway Administration. Closing the bridge was destined to adversely effect businesses in Eastport. Without the bridge, folks wanting to travel to downtown Annapolis would have an annoying detour through suburbs such as Westwinds and Knightsbridge. Not likely!

So the Eastport business community fought back. Just as the State of Maryland severed the road link to the Eastport Peninsula, the local business community decided to sever political ties. Secession! Eastport may well have looked south for a precedent, as the Conch Republic in Florida took

INDEPENDENCE FOR EASTPORT

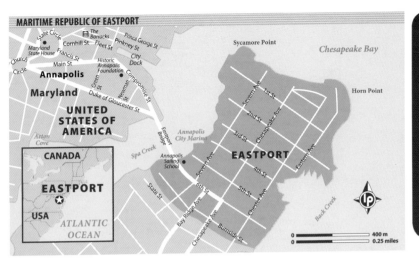

similar steps for similar reasons in the early 1980s (see Conch Republic, p130).

According to the official history of the republic: 'So the Maritime Republic of Eastport was founded on Super Bowl Sunday, 1998, when patriots residing on the Horn Point peninsula rose up in revolt against the snobbish suppression of "Annapolis Proper" across the harbor.'

Nine groups, calling themselves the Chowderhead Eastport Militia, gathered at the southern end of the bridge on Sunday 25 January 1998, armed with muskets and four cannons. Cannon fire was returned from the Annapolis side. The Unanimous Declaration of Independence was read by Eastport poet laureate Jeff Holland. It was, of course, (mostly) all in fun (see Unanimous Declaration of Independence, p118).

The secession was a success. Businesses in Eastport actually saw an increase in trade, and the Maritime Republic organisers reportedly made over US$20,000 from the sale of flags and other souvenirs. Since the declaration in 1998, however, the Maritime Republic of Eastport has not followed the pattern established by most micronations. They're not in the currency-and-stamp business, preferring to dedicate their time and efforts to the social good through various fundraising initiatives.

According to official figures, over a million people a year visit Annapolis. And it's fair to say that hardly any of them know that they're only minutes away from a breakaway republic. The people of the Maritime Republic of Eastport differ only slightly from their neighbours across the bridge in the USA. Aside from a slightly more developed sense of humour, and a noticeably increased appetite for crabs and beer, you'd struggle to tell them apart at all.

PEOPLE & CULTURE

According to MRE Premier – and all-round nice person – Jessica Pachler, the primary impetus behind the formation of the republic was to foster a spirit of independence and merriment, and at the same time, to celebrate Eastport's proud heritage and quality of life.

> Now that the MRE has successfully established its independence and aided the prosperity of Eastport's businesses, it has directed its attention on ensuring that the MRE remains one of the best places to live ANYWHERE! We are committed to improving the quality of life here and hold numerous FUN charitable events to benefit needy organisations.

The Maritime Republic of Eastport has raised almost US$200,000 for charitable causes.

FESTIVALS & EVENTS

TUG-OF-WAR

The famous Tug-of-War (also known as the 'Slaughter Across the Water') was established in 1998, and has been contested

ALL EYES ON THE TUG

UNANIMOUS DECLARATION OF INDEPENDENCE

This is an edited version of Eastport's Declaration of Independence.

When in the course of Public Works it becomes necessary to dismantle the Bridge connecting the Eastport Peninsula with the Annapolis Mainland, it is fitting that we, the People of the Neighborhood of Eastport, also dismantle and by doing so dissolve the social, economic and political bands as well as the physical bands which have connected us.

We hold these truths to be self evident, that all men and women are created equal as evidenced by the fact that, no matter their social or economic status, they all wear the same beat-up deck shoes. That they are endowed by their Creator with certain inalienable rights, that among these are Life, Liberty, and the Pursuit of Happiness. That is to say, to get a life and enjoy our Work as well as the jovial companionship of Family and Friends; Liberty from suits, ties and socks; and the Pursuit of prize Rockfish, the Finish Gun, two-week cruises, Crabs, Beer and Oysters...

Therefore we now Declare our Independence and thereby do celebrate the unique maritime Character of our own Culture, our own History, our own Heritage, our own Horticulture, Architecture and Naval Architecture, our People and our Retrievers and Felines, our own Neighborhood, our own Eastport!

We, therefore, the representatives of the Maritime Republic of Eastport do solemnly declare that this Neighborhood is, and by Rights ought to be a Free and Independent State, that we are Absolved from all Allegiances to Annapolis Proper, and that we have full Power to levy War, conclude Peace, contract Alliances, establish Commerce, and do all the other Stuff which Independent States may of right do, especially to throw really big Parties. And for the support of this Declaration, with a firm reliance on the fact that nobody's ever going to take us too seriously anyway, we mutually pledge to each other our Lives, our Fortunes, and our Sacred Sense of Humor.

between forces from the republic and neighbouring Annapolis annually ever since. Official Maritime Republic sources, commenting on the second tug-of-war in 1999, claim that 'surveyors discovered afterward that the competitors tugged so hard that the Eastport peninsula is now 2.1403m closer to City Dock than it was before the first tug'. The rope is over 500m long, and is tugged at by almost 500 people.

AMBASSADOR'S BALL

The annual Ambassador's Ball is held in late January, and coincides with the anniversary of the founding of the breakaway republic. It also serves as a celebration for those successfully appointed to the MRE governing body. The ball, a glittering affair, is also one of the main fundraising events on the calendar. In 2006, for example, the ball raised money for the Displaced Musicians of New Orleans charity.

BRIDGE RUN

Visitors should look out for the annual '0.5km Eastport Bridge Run' (note the Republic's use of metric measurement here), a blistering race across the infamous bridge.

FACTS FOR THE VISITOR

PLACES TO STAY

Peninsula House (☎ 410-267 8796; 11 Chester Ave, Eastport; d from US$165) Eastport is lovely. Which is

why there are lots of B&Bs to stay at and hardly any awful motels. For lovely rooms, beautiful gardens and a real sense of the republic, the Peninsula House is a fine choice. A white picket fence and three spic-and-span heritage rooms greet the visitor. The highlight of your stay will surely be the gourmet breakfast, which might include drunken crab strata, stout and gouda pancakes with lemon butter crab Benedict, or something equally divine. And champagne! The well-travelled owners are active members of the republic and are a wealth of information for activities in the MRE, and across the border in Annapolis too. If you're lucky enough to be arriving at the docks by boat, the Peninsula House offers a pick-up service.

Inn at Horn Point (☎ 410 268-1126; 100 Chesapeake Ave, Eastport; d from US$140) Conveniently located just a block from the Severn River, the Inn at Horn Point is a 100-year-old house offering five neat rooms, all with bathrooms, cable TV and balconies.

PROUD PARTICIPANTS SPRINT ACROSS THE INFAMOUS ANNAPOLIS–EASTPORT BRIDGE

ELECTED HEADS OF STATE AT WAR: MRE PREMIER JESSICA PACHLER AND MARYLAND GOVERNOR BOB EHRLICH TUG IT OUT BEFORE THE MAIN EVENT

Inn at Spa Creek (☎ 410 263-8866; 417 Severn Ave, Eastport; d from US$160) Just off the bridge in Eastport is this bright, modern guesthouse, featuring three double rooms. Close to the water taxi for those wishing to cross the border into the USA to visit Annapolis, the Inn does not allow small children and is strictly nonsmoking.

PLACES TO EAT

Eastport Yacht Club (EYC; ☎ 410 267-9549; 317 First St, Eastport) With over 500 members, the EYC is a principal community hub in the republic. Dinner is available from 4.30pm most nights. Check out taco night on a Sunday. Yum.

Chart House (☎ 410 268-7166; 300 Second St, Eastport) A popular dining spot for members of the Maritime Republic's elite, Chart House serves brunch, lunch and dinner with a heavy emphasis on seafood. But it's the views across Spa Creek to Annapolis that lift Eastport's incarnation of this American chain restaurant out of mediocrity.

Wild Orchid Café (☎ 410 268-8009; 909 Bay Ridge Ave, Eastport; mains around US$30) Declared the best meal in Annapolis by the *Baltimore Sun*, this restaurant is a fancy fine dining option. With regionally inspired, innovative dishes such as crab fondue, tuna with rice noodles and ginger-infused pork, the Wild Orchid will leave you toasting the republic.

O'Learys Seafood Restaurant (☎ 410 263-0884; 310 Third St, Eastport; mains around US$28) King of Eastport's 'Restaurant Row', O'Leary's is a favourite of visitors and locals. Along with their famous crab cakes, O'Leary's also takes a walk on the wild side with dishes such as Thai barbecued *mahi mahi* with macadamia shrimp.

PLACES TO SHOP

Artful Dogs (☎ 410 263-4994; 614 Burnside St, Eastport) Artful Dogs is possibly Eastport's premier supplier of functional art for dogs. Architect-designed doghouses and tasteful portraits of your pooch are on offer. A must.

THINGS TO SEE & DO

Annapolis Maritime Museum (☎ 410 295-0104; cnr Second St & Back Creek, Eastport; admission free; ☽ afternoons Sat & Sun, other times by appointment) Following Hurricane Isabel in 2003, the Maritime Museum was forced to operate from a temporary location, but the museum's Barge House location was finally opened in late 2005. That an Annapolis museum should operate in the Maritime Republic of Eastport is a quirk of history, and a dash of good fortune: the exhibitions and special events celebrating the region's vital links with the sea have been educating Eastportians and Americans for over 40 years.

GETTING THERE & AWAY

Starting from State Circle in central Annapolis, it's about four minutes' travel by car to get to the Maritime Republic of Eastport. Heading south, School St, Duke of Gloucester St and Compromise St will get you to Spa Creek, which is the border with the Maritime Republic. Continue driving across the bridge (Sixth St) and turn left into Chesapeake Ave and you will find yourself right in the heart of the Republic. The total distance is just under one mile.

REPUBLIC OF RATHNELLY

A lovely pocket of downtown Toronto, Canada, the Republic of Rathnelly was founded in 1967 to coincide with Canada's centenary celebrations. With tongue firmly in cheek, residents of the neighbourhood were issued with passports and invited to take part in elections. The tight-knit neighbourhood still celebrates with a bi-annual street party along Rathnelly Ave in June. The 40th anniversary party in 2007 will be one to watch!

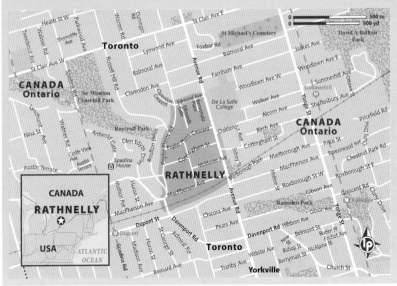

Republic of Saugeais

As you might expect from a micronation in France, Saugeais has more pedigree than most, with a history dating back to the Middle Ages. Like all good micronations it started with a joke that's kept Saugets and tourists sniggering while raising funds to maintain one of Europe's sweetest abbeys.

LOCATION

Saugeais is in the upper valley of the River Doubs near France's border with Switzerland, in an area known as Val Sauget since the Middle Ages.

FACTS ABOUT SAUGEAIS

WEBSITE www.otcm25.org/republique_du_saugeais .htm (in French)

FOUNDED 1947

HEAD OF STATE President Georgette Bertin-Pourchet, elected in 2006

CAPITAL Montbenoît

LANGUAGE French

NATIONAL DAY First Sunday in October

CURRENCY Saugeais Sol (rare) and the Euro

AREA Roughly 1000 sq km

ARMED FORCES 13 in 2005

HISTORY

During the 12th century the Lord of Joux decided to flaunt his power and curry favour with God by building an abbey in the upper reaches of the valley of Doubs. Monks arrived to help construction and they took such a shine to the local hermit, Benoît, that they decided to name the building after him. The abbey remained under the authority of the Lords of Joux, who kept such a low profile that nobody bothered to take the abbey off them until it closed its doors in 1723.

Fast forward to post-war France when a visiting government official lunches at Georges Pourchet's Hôtel de l'Abbaye in Montbenoît and starts chatting with his amiable host. It must have been a slow business day, because Georges cheekily asked the official if he had a pass to visit the Free Republic of Saugeais, a historical invention of the hotel owner. The official, perhaps enjoying a little too much of an *après* lunch brandy, found himself saying: 'A republic must have a president. You are appointed president of the Free Republic of Saugeais.' And with that the Pourchet dynasty was born.

George Pourchet served as president until his death in 1968 and his wife, Gabrielle, retired from running the hotel not long after his passing to help restore the abbey. In 1972 to help raise funds for the abbey's restoration a small festival began and over lunch the townspeople talked over the old story of the republic, eventually electing Gabrielle president. She was a much-loved ruler, who worked hard for charity and was honoured with her image on the national banknote. Neighbouring France made her Knight of the Legion of Honour in 1977 and she worked tirelessly until her death in 2005. A heartfelt funeral at the abbey she helped to restore included the singing of the national anthem by a local fire brigade. In 2006 a new president, Georgette Bertin-Pourchet, was elected to carry on the legacy.

GEOGRAPHY

The 1000-sq-km republic is broken up into a staggering 11 municipalities: Les Alliés, Arçon, Bugny, La Chaux-de-Gilley, Gilley, Hauterive-la-Fresne, la Longeville, Maisons-du-Bois-Lièvremont, Montbenoît, Montflovin and Ville-du-Pont.

THE MUCH-LOVED FORMER PRESIDENT SHOWS OFF THE NATIONAL FLAG

Montbenoît, the capital, is tiny, but the small township of Gilley, which locals somewhat facetiously call the 'the republic's economic capital', serves as a hub.

GOVERNMENT & POLITICS

Presidents are elected by townsfolk in a relatively harmonious process with usually only one candidate. There have been two democratic elections (1972 and 2006) with a French government appointment in 1947.

PEOPLE & CULTURE

With a population of roughly 4500 citizens this country may not be up there with that other great Franco pocket-nation, Andorra (population 67,000), but it's well ahead of the Holy See (population 1000).

Generally people are country folk – even the capital city of Montbenoît barely has more than a couple of hundred residents.

FACTS FOR THE VISITOR

PLACES TO STAY & EAT

Both Gilley and Montbenoît have limited places to stay, which can often be booked up by the passing ski crowd. **Hotel des Voyageurs** (☎ 03 8138 1085; Montbenoît) and **Hotel du Commerce** (☎ 03 8143 3087; Gilley) both offer meals and accommodation.

SHOPPING

There's no special shopping to be done in this quarter of provincial France, except on the national holiday when markets crowd Montbenoît's main street selling all manner of local handicrafts from knitwear to pottery.

THINGS TO SEE & DO

Obviously the main attraction in Montbenoît is the **abbey**, which dominates the village both architecturally and culturally. Montbenoît Abbey was built during the 12th century with the soaring cloisters added in the 15th century. The wooden sculptured choir stalls are another highlight.

Perched on a hill, **Chateau de Joux** is a genuine Middle Ages castle complete with three moats and a drawbridge. The fort was rebuilt in 1879, but it was here that the original order to build Montbenoît Abbey was sent out.

Further into the Jura Mountains, there are several downhill and cross-country ski areas including Métabief Mont d'Or, a resort made up of six smaller villages.

GETTING THERE & AWAY

There are regular buses to large regional centres such as Pontarlier, approximately seven hours from Paris. The nearest international airport is in Geneva.

To enter the republic, you must buy a *laissez-passer*, a pass emblazoned with ribbons and the national seal, which may be pinned on you by the president herself.

OVERSEEING THE BORDER PATROL WITH ONE OF SAUGEAIS' CRACK TROOPS

TOTO, I DON'T THINK WE'RE IN KANSAS ANY MORE

During the 1992 US presidential election – the one that swept Bill Clinton to power – the subject at the top of the political agenda in western Kansas was not foreign policy or healthcare...it was secession!

A referendum question was placed on the ballot papers in several counties asking whether citizens wanted to secede from the US, to avoid paying a state levy for public schools. The referendum passed overwhelmingly, but – despite petitions to both the US Congress and the UN – Western Kansas, in all its glory, is still where it always was.

Barony of Caux

Motto: *Deus Pascit Corvus* (God Feeds the Raven)

Monarchies are few and far between in the 21st century. Most have been eclipsed by democracy and quietly wait on the sidelines doing the odd bit of charity work in between Christmas addresses and ceremonial openings. Not so for the Barony of Caux, which boasts over 100 subjects and has just begun its own TV station. All from a European aristocracy that is now based in downtown Toronto, Canada.

LOCATION

Although they claim territory in Shropshire, UK, and Normandy, France, the best place to catch up with the baron is at the embassy in Toronto, Canada.

FACTS ABOUT BARONY OF CAUX

ADDRESS Barony of Caux Embassy, 129 Barton Ave, Toronto, Canada M6G 1R1

WEBSITE www.baronyofcaux.com

FOUNDED AD 1069 (Grand Restitution 2001)

HEAD OF STATE Baron John Corbett

LANGUAGE English

POPULATION Almost 100

NATIONAL SPORT Whacking the Welsh

NATIONAL HYMN Overture to 'Tannhauser' by Wagner

EMBASSIES Toronto (see address above), Canada; Hérault, France and several consulates

HISTORY

According to the barony, William the Conqueror first gave Roger Fitzcorbet a parcel of land and a title way back in 1069. Fitzcorbet was born in Normandy (modern France) in an ancestral property known as Pays de Caux and benefited from William's invasion of England with new territory around modern Shropshire. The name became Corbet and the dynasty thrived, building Caus Castle, which included a market and a chapel. The dynasty's reign was interrupted by the Black Death, which wiped out many of the local people including the Corbets. The last recorded person living in the castle was in 1645.

For many centuries the barony was vacant until a Canadian communications consultant, John Corbett, lay claim to the title. In 2001 Corbett staged what became known as the Grand Restitution and became the 39th Baron of Caux with claims on land in Shropshire and France. Peers were also appointed from Corbett's immediate family including Lady Deborah and the heir apparent, Lord Patrick of Caudebec, whose interests are listed on the royal website as 'women, Stolichnaya, bizarre dentistry and recreational self-abuse'.

In 2003 the barony was rocked when the Lord Chancellor, Lord Ratlinghope, was caught, according to the *Baronial Broadsheet*, with 'one hand in the baronial exchequer and one hand up the skirt of a baronial serving wench'. Subsequently, his lordship was deemed too 'skanky' to continue serving the barony.

GEOGRAPHY

Currently the barony's territory consists of 186 sq metres of downtown Toronto, but claims additional territories in France and the UK.

GOVERNMENT & POLITICS

The barony proclaims that it is the only feudal government in the 21st century with an absolute ruler. Furthermore, the baron asserts that 'experiments in governance (democracy, communism, empire, global commerce) are deficient, and lead eventually to ruin, out of which rises, once again, feudal governance'.

A little huffy that baronial forces have not been called on for recent UN actions in Iraq, the baron sees the Welsh as a traditional rival who may still incur on his borders. To combat this threat, the national sport of Welsh whacking is encouraged at national celebrations such as Commons Day (1 June) and Restitution Day (27 August).

Consulates abound with baronial consular officials promised the power to 'ignore tickets, jury duty and other civic duty' plus a racy red Barony of Caux Diplomatic Corp polo shirt. For only US$20, honorary consuls have sprung up in Reno, USA, and Bangkok, Thailand.

PEOPLE & CULTURE

Known variously as Caletans and Cauxinards, the people of the barony are a mostly peaceful lot except where their natural enemies the Welsh are concerned. There was some speculation (mostly in the *Baronial Broadsheet*) about the barony creating weapons of mass destruction in an undisclosed location in France. The armoury is being developed in response to the Welsh experimenting with battering rams and slingshots, but weapons probably include a trebuchet, onager and the aptly named two-testicled brioca. 'We don't like to think of this as escalation', says Brigadier Stephen Galpin of the Militia of Caux, 'but the Barony of Caux will never be the last to defend its home manors, if you know what I mean'.

The barony produces a semi-annual update called the *Baronial Broadsheet*, which includes announcements of new citizenry. Also featured in the emailed update are advertisements for everything from volunteers to test bullet-proof vests to a new lord chancellor who must be 'taller than Kofi Annan and smarter than George W Bush'.

The barony has recently begun work in TV by founding the Baronial Broadcast Corporation (BBC). At the time of research, the range of broadcast extended as much as 90m from the embassy and programming consisted principally of a static-stormed aspect of the Grand Staircase of the Baronial Embassy in Toronto.

FESTIVALS & EVENTS

The biggest festival of the year is **Commons Day** (usually held on 1 June, though it has been moved in the past in order to host the event in the French embassy). Often celebrated with roast boar and foaming mead, the event always includes a round of traditional whacking of the Welsh.

THE NOBLE EDIFICE OF THE EMBASSY OF CAUX IN DOWNTOWN TORONTO

Nobles and knights are later investitured by the baron himself.

By contrast **Restitution Day** (27 August) is a more sombre event, reserved for reflection on the state of the barony and remembering the absent King William (of the conquering fame). This is usually followed by what the *Baronial Broadsheet* calls 'drinking, wenching, belching and falling down that has become so much the hallmark of this sacred day'.

FACTS FOR THE VISITOR

SHOPPING

The barony trades with subjects and nobles. As well as consulates (US$20 with red polo shirt), the barony also offers passports (CAD$50), which are endorsed by the baron himself and allow safe passage throughout the barony.

THINGS TO SEE & DO

The claimed territories of the barony in Shropshire and Normandy include several picturesque attractions including **Castle Caus** and the majestic **Chateau of Caux**, though these lands are still in the hands of the British and the French. The sole undisputed territory of the Barony is the **Toronto Embassy** (www.baronyofcaux.com; 129 Barton Ave, Toronto), which is known for its gardens planted with wildflowers native to Caux, France.

GETTING THERE & AWAY

The barony's embassy is located in downtown Toronto on Barton Ave, which is parallel to Bloor St W. While passports are not essential, they will help with identification of citizens and may ensure a cup of tea.

IMAGINE

While not exactly a nation – it had no land – John Lennon's declaration of a new nation called Nutopia – at a press conference on April Fool's Day 1973 – certainly attracted attention. Lennon and partner Yoko Ono declared that Nutopia had 'cosmic' laws, an all-white flag and existed to embody the ideals in Lennon's iconic song 'Imagine'. The pair also answered questions about the deportation notice Lennon had received earlier that week from the Immigration and Naturalization Service, demanding he leave the USA.

The Nutopian National Anthem – several seconds of silence designed to allow the listener to recall their favourite song – appeared on Lennon and Ono's 'Mind Games' album, along with sleeve notes that outlined details about the new country. Lennon also had an 'Embassy of Nutopia' plaque on his apartment wall in New York City.

CYBER NERDS UNITE

When micronations gained some attention in the 1980s, it was bit of an effort to start one up. A common course of action was to declare your bedroom a new nation, but then there would be the inevitable diplomatic crisis with mum about her just wandering in without a passport.

Another common course was to claim a bit of land that no-one wanted, or that was in dispute. But that proved to be even more of a drag, given the lengthy legal battles with 'the Man' that would invariably follow – not to mention physical battles. The annals of micronationalism are filled with instances of macronations invading micronations in an attempt to wrest land back from the grasp of various 'toy emperors'. Big trouble can ensue, especially if you follow the creed of Erwin S Strauss in his book *How to Start Your Own Country* (1979), where he advocates the 'mouse that roared' strategy for start-up nations. In essence, this means obtaining a 'basement nuke' and threatening to use it against invaders (obviously, Strauss was writing pre-9/11).

Clearly, battling mum or detonating bombs is not for everyone. But with the rise of the Internet, all that has changed. Now anyone with Internet access can lay claim to his or her own 'virtual territory'.

Because of this unfettered access, many micronationalists think that virtual micronations are purely for kids, egomaniacs and scammers, but others attach real significance to the phenomenon. The State of Sabotage (p148) champions the notion that 'America is not a geographic place, but rather a concept'. Thus, goes the argument in an extremely simplified form, starting up a virtual nation is as valid as founding the world's largest superpower. The current nature of geopolitics seems to back this up, too, with more than a few analysts claiming that a 'real' nation's most valuable commodity is no longer land but the fluidity of its economy (with governmental offices in one country, means of production in another, and customers in yet another).

Whatever the philosophy, it seems there's a virtual nation tailored to every taste: it might be filled with role-playing Dungeons & Dragons freaks; it could be a nation of John Wayne fanatics; a population of dope smokers; or a citizenry of David Crosby fans (shudder). The list is boundless.

Before you travel these uncharted waters, though, take our advice. Beware of any micronation hosted on a free server such as Geocities – you'll be bombarded with an avalanche of spam and popup windows before you've had a chance to click on the coat of arms. Generally, if a nation can't afford its own domain name, then it's not really worthy of further investigation.

Even though the idea of virtual nations seems to be a fad whose time has passed (especially considering the net no longer has the novelty value it originally did), it's still worth checking out perhaps the two best-known virtual states.

These examples (one going strong and one defunct, but with an enduring legend) take the fluid nature of the Internet and make it mean something deep and profound (or at least genuinely funny).

STATE OF NSK

MOTTO 'Art is Fanaticism that Demands Diplomacy' **AREA** Time

WEBSITE www.nskstate.com **POPULATION** 'More than the Vatican'

HEAD OF STATE
Imminent-consistent
spirit

GOVERNMENT
Collective Absolutism

CURRENCY NSK

LANGUAGE The body

The NSK State is a wing of Neue Slowenische Kunst (German for 'New Slovenian Art'), a Slovenian art collective that also includes among its ranks the well-known shock-rock-techno-pomp band Laibach. The entire Neue Slowenische Kunst movement has continually attracted controversy for its use and recontextualisation of totalitarian imagery, incorporating it into surreal artistic settings that invariably comment on the incongruities of modern-day statehood.

Fittingly, then, in 1991 the collective formed their own micronation, known simply as the State of NSK. This virtual state issues its own passports and postage stamps and has had temporary embassies in Moscow, Berlin and Sarajevo. There's a bit of conceptual doublespeak to the whole exercise: according to official propaganda, 'NSK confers the status of a state not to territory but to mind, whose borders are in a state of flux, in accordance with the movements and changes of its symbolic and physical collective body'. And there's no human king or head of state, just the 'collective' – a temporal body of citizens who materialise 'within the space of any pre-existing state, in peaceful co-existence'.

Having sprung from an art collective, there's a bit more to NSK than your standard virtual micronation. Events, happenings, performances and global gallery exhibitions (often described as 'temporary embassies') are all a part of this state's unique interaction with the physical world.

LIZBEKISTAN (DEFUNCT)

MOTTO Optimism During the Crisis

WEBSITE www.lizbekistan.com/index2.htm (archival); www.lizvegas.com (a place for homeless Lizbekians to caress their nipples)

HEAD OF STATE Princess Liz

CURRENCY The Nipple (value pegged to the price of a packet of Marlboro cigarettes)

AREA Virtual

POPULATION Thousands

Lizbekistan rode the wave of virtual micronations of the late 1990s to become possibly the most popular cyber state, with a population in the thousands. Founded by Australian artist Liz Sterling, Lizbekistan was a highly irreverent exercise but also complex, imaginative and conceptual. At its peak Lizbekistan was home to four newspapers including the *Dependent* (motto: 'The Voice of Authority') and printed its own currency, stamps and passports.

Like NSK, Stirling was motivated by a serious desire to examine citizenship, community and the notion of statehood – and to mock the real world of nation states and all its heavy symbolism. But whereas NSK chose irony and a sense of humour that's not immediately obvious to convey its message, Stirling embraced lowbrow comedy and an obsession with the nipples of its citizens (the Lizebekistanian currency was the Nipple, often the cue for an onslaught of Benny Hill–style jokes).

Stirling 'blew up' Lizbekistan on 9/9/99 – on that date the website faded to pink and was no more. That meant thousands of Lizbekians were 'homeless' and for a while Stirling maintained the Lizbekdiaspora site to accommodate them until that, too, faded away.

But the legend of Lizbekistan lingers on, and its citizens still remain moist-eyed whenever Princess Liz's name is evoked.

FURTHER READING

- **Amorph!03: Summit of Micronations** (www.muu.fi/amorph03/impressum.html) The first Summit of Micronations was held in Helsinki, Finland, in 2003 as part of the 7th Amorph! performance art biennale. It engaged in a philosophical discussion of what it means to be a micronation, leavened with a particular strain of northern European mock-seriousness. The summit featured mainly virtual nations (and is therefore recommended for anyone interested in this area, even if it is 100% Euro-centric), including NSK and the Transnational Republic, along with Sealand. The curators of the summit, Tellervo Kalleinen and Oliver Kochta, published a comprehensive book of the proceedings, *Summit of Micronations/Protocols*, which included case studies, essays and artists' contributions. A second summit is planned for 2007.

Conch Republic

Motto: We Seceded Where Others Failed

The Conch Republic is a light-hearted secessionist state, formed by local business leaders and politicians in protest over treatment by the US Federal government. It shares certain foundation similarities with the Maritime Republic of Eastport, which formed in Annapolis in 1998.

Founded in 1982, the Conch Republic is still going strong, using humour and goodwill to make the lives of its citizens and participants better. This attitude is seen to good effect in the nation's foreign affairs policy: 'The mitigation of world tension through the exercise of humor.'

LOCATION

The Conch Republic lays claim to the whole Florida Keys area, a 220km stretch of islands in the southeastern USA. Encompassing all land south of Skeeter's Last Chance Saloon, just south of Florida City, the republic occupies sun-kissed land contested by the state of Florida on behalf of the USA. The Capitol is located on Key West at the southern tip of the long stretch of islands. This island, measuring about 6km by 4km reportedly has the largest number of bars *and* churches per capita in North America.

FACTS ABOUT THE CONCH REPUBLIC

POSTAL ADDRESS Office of the Secretary General, PO Box 658, Key West, FL/CR 33041 – 6583

TELEPHONE ☎ 305-296-0213

WEBSITE www.conchrepublic.com

FOUNDED 23 April 1982

HISTORY

In April 1982, the US border patrol set up a military-style roadblock outside the Last Chance Saloon on the Overseas Hwy in Florida City. All traffic heading north from the string of islands known as the Florida Keys was stopped and searched for illegal immigrants and drugs. The traffic jam stretched 28km. National media were alerted to this unprecedented 'border patrol' on US soil, and the mayor of Key West, Dennis Wardlow, also pricked up his ears.

As news of the checkpoint spread, businesses in the Keys noticed an immediate drop in customers. Day trips declined and holiday-makers cancelled bookings. Mayor Wardlow headed to Miami in an attempt to get an injunction against the 'blockade'. He failed. As he left the court house, he announced to waiting media, 'Tomorrow at noon the Florida Keys will secede from the Union!'

The Conch Republic was formed, with the Keys seceding from the US at a ceremony in Mallory Square, Key West. Conch Republic officials declared war on the US,

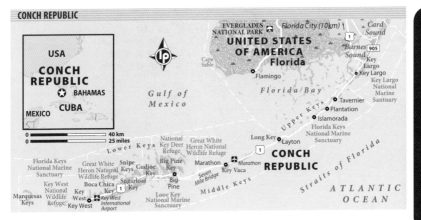

immediately surrendered and then lodged applications for a billion dollars in foreign aid to restore the local 'post-war' economy. This ingenious plan went entirely ignored by federal and Florida state officials. For the media and locals, however, it was a winning strategy.

Conch Republic affairs continued to gather momentum over the next 15 years, with highlights including a starring role at the Summit of the Americas in Miami in 1994 (the republic's officials somehow managed to get a room at the official hotel on the same floor as the Canadian prime minister), where they were ultimately successful in spreading their message of goodwill. The following year, based on their positive presence at the summit, Conch Republic officials received an official invitation to 1995's Florida Jubilee. 1995 also saw the republic on alert, following a threatened invasion by US forces. Thankfully, the situation was resolved and the nations continued to co-exist peacefully (see The Great Invasion of '95, p133).

Late in 1996 the Conch Republic again stole headlines when they promoted the fact that, despite the federal government shutting down for several days over budget disagreements, the Conch Republic remained open for business. Part of their press release read, 'We realize that the shutdown in Washington may further delay processing of the foreign aid we requested from Washington in 1982, but since we have been waiting for fourteen years, a few more days or weeks won't matter.'

A month later, government services were again shut down. This time, with the local tourism industry suffering, the Conch Republic swung into action with another masterful plan. Popular recreation area Fort Jefferson was closed due to the government having no money to pay staff. Leaders of the Conch Republic raised the money to pay the wages – thus making it possible for boats to operate in the area, but were unable to get either the state or federal governments to agree to reopen the Fort.

An attorney friend of the Conch Republic's king decided to weigh in. He wanted to take the government to court (knowing the media attention would force a backdown), but first had to engineer some civil disobedience; Conch's secretary general hired a light aircraft and flew down to Fort Jefferson, delivered a cheque for wages and declared the fort open in the name of the Conch Republic. The anticipated citation for illegally entering a closed federal facility was duly served, and the case – The United States of America versus Peter Anderson – went to federal court.

When the case was called a few months later, the federal government was suddenly in a big hurry to drop the case. The republic had demonstrated how adept it was at protecting its citizens.

Conch Republic mastermind, Secretary General Peter Anderson, has travelled extensively in the region using only his Conch Republic passport. Indeed, the Conch Republic passport, diplomats and general citizens have been accepted by 13 Caribbean Nations (including Cuba) in addition to Mexico and six European nations.

PEOPLE & CULTURE

The Conch Republic prides itself on leading the world in a number of socially progressive policy positions. It mandates that its citizens respect and obey traditions as well as laws, meaning that long-held beliefs and ways of living are enshrined and accepted.

Further, the republic claims to be the world's only operating meritocracy. Anyone who sees that something needs to be done, and possesses the skills to do it, can do so secure in the knowledge that they will be recognised in that position. Indeed, many of the republic's senior positions are held because of this understanding.

FESTIVALS & EVENTS

NATIONAL DAY CELEBRATIONS

Any traveller in or near the Conch Republic in late April would be crazy not to join in the festivities, which seem to get bigger and more elaborate each year. In recent years, the Conch Republic's national celebrations have involved events that take place over more than one week.

While the calendar is ever-changing, regular events include a kick-off party, a drag race, elections and investiture of a king, the so-called 'world's longest parade' down Duval St, the annual naval battle for the Conch Republic (pitting the republic's vessels against the invading federal ships of the US coast guard) and the annual ball. Most events involve a fundraising component, with charities helped in recent years including Helpline, the Foster Children's Fund and AIDS Help, Inc. Check the Conch Republic website for details of the next event.

PASSPORTS

Regular citizen passports are available from the **Conch Republic Passport Control office** (405 Petronia, Suite 2, Key West, FL/CR 33040). Alternatively, an application form is available from the republic's website. Passports for regular citizens are US$200 for residents of the USA and Canada, and an extra $18 for orders from other nations.

Diplomatic passports are also available. Goodwill ambassador passports – the cheapest – cost US$900, while ambassador passports cost US$10,000. Applicants for ambassador passports must live in the capital city of their country of residence, and – as well as coughing up a fair chunk of change – must be able to demonstrate the ability to genuinely represent the Conch Republic at the highest levels.

FACTS FOR THE VISITOR

PLACES TO STAY

Angelina Guest House (☎ 305-294 4480; 302 Angela St, Key West; d US$95) There is no shortage of

YES, WE DO SERVE LOBSTER!

THE GREAT INVASION OF '95

When, in September 1995, news filtered through that the 478th Civil Affairs Battalion of the US Army Reserve was planning to conduct training exercises on land claimed by the Conch Republic, Conch officials sent a letter of protest to President Bill Clinton, the Joint Chiefs, the Secretary of State and others.

The 478th was also contacted and informed of the Conch Republic's 'war footing' following their breach of international protocols. Conch officials told the battalion that they intended to repel the assault. The army was, needless to say, gobsmacked.

Major Muller from the 478th called the republic leaders to insist that he represented the 'good guys', but the Conch Republic was unmoved. It sent a list of demands, or, rather, one demand: that the army should ask for permission to enter when they reached the border. Less than an hour later, a fax was received on US Army letterhead acquiescing to the demands and stating that the army 'in no way meant to challenge or impugn the sovereignty of the Conch Republic'. Recognition!

The following day, hundreds of Conch Republic citizens assembled at the northern border as the army trucks rolled ever-closer. Admiral Harvey of the Conch Republic blocked the path of the army. Major Kim Hooper from the US Army approached. The list of demands was read, to which Hooper replied, 'Yes Ma'am'. Permission was sought and granted, and an invasion became a friendly visit.

accommodation options for folks on vacation, although the big-city variety is often matched by big-city 'charm'. One lovely option, however, is this restored Victorian-era guesthouse; it's one step up from a hostel in price, hospitality and ambience. It features a pool, garden and continental breakfast.

The Mermaid & the Alligator (☎ 305-294 1894; 729 Truman Ave, Key West) For those able to splash out a little, this beautiful Victorian building comes with period trimmings, friendly staff, wrap-around porches, a pool and breakfast served in the garden, all from around US$180.

PLACES TO EAT & DRINK

Schooner Wharf Bar (☎ 305-292 3302; 202 William St, Key West) The focal point for most big Conch Republic celebrations is this slightly ramshackle bar at the bottom of William St overlooking the Land's End Marina. Comfortable unpretentious surroundings and food to match, with burgers at around $7 and Cuban-style fresh fish a mouth-watering $15.

The Schooner Wharf Bar hosts regular live music on its small stage and many other events through the year, including the **Lowering of the Pirate Wench** – where a woman is lowered from the mast of the schooner *Liberty Clipper* – at midnight on New Year's Eve.

Hog's Breath Bar (☎ 305-292 2032; 400 Front St, Key West) With a motto 'Better than no breath at all', the Hog's Breath has a fantastic location opposite Mallory Sq, making it a perfect spot to watch the sun go down. Sip a margarita, treat yourself to the raw bar (fresh seafood) and enjoy the live music every day with the regular party-hard crowd.

THINGS TO SEE

MALLORY SQUARE

On the west coast of Key West, this small ocean-front square is the hub of the tight-knit community, and a drawcard for visitors from the US and beyond. The cobblestoned square is the site of Key West's famous sunset celebrations, and is also the focus of many Conch Republic events. Jugglers, buskers and craft markets are the order of the day (and night), and the square is also home to the 50,000-gallon **Key West Aquarium**.

HEMINGWAY HOUSE

Celebrated author Ernest Hemingway lived large in Key West from 1929 until he moved to Havana, Cuba, in 1939. He lived in this handsome **house** (☎ 305-294 1575; 907 Whitehead St, Key West) for eight of those years. Guided tours around the house and grounds, taking in the lush swimming pool and the disconcerting quantity of roaming cats, costs US$8.

CONCH TOUR TRAIN

For almost fifty years, the **Conch Tour Train** (☎ 305-294 5161; 501 & 302 Front St, Key West; adult/child $25/12) has been tootling along the streets of Key West, giving visitors a

PEOPLE RELAXING ON SUNSET PIER, KEY WEST

90-minute snapshot of paradise. Hop aboard and take an expert tour around the key, taking in Mallory Sq, Sloppy Joe's, the City Cemetery, Hemingway House and many other points of interest.

GETTING THERE & AWAY

The easiest way to get there is to first reach Florida's biggest city and main hub, Miami. From here, many fly directly to Key West, although the trip down Hwy 1 (known as the Overseas Hwy, and featuring 43 bridges) is a great way to explore the Conch Republic's 'Northern Territories'. Unless you're interrupted by an accident or a traffic jam (one road in, one road out) the trip from Miami will take you about three-and-a-half hours. Bus services also run regularly for about US$35.

KINGDOM OF L'ANSE-SAINT-JEAN

Snug on the southern shore of the stunning Saguenay Fjord, about 250km north of Quebec City in Canada, L'Anse-Saint-Jean is a beautiful town in a beautiful part of the world. Founded in 1838, the town grew on the back of lumber, maple syrup and fishing (salmon was an easy catch). Nobody would have guessed that the secessionist bug would breed so healthily here in this quiet, polite, stable society of 1600 people.

And yet, on 21 January 1997, a referendum was passed in this small town creating North America's first self-declared 'municipal monarchy'. There was a distinct religious overtone to the declaration: upon his ascension to the throne, King Denys proclaimed 'I vow to be a very Christian king, defender of God and His churches', and one of the stated aims of the nation was to fund a project to sculpt a 1-sq-km face of John the Baptist into nearby Mt Edward.

All the same, the king's commitment to art projects and the desire to create a tourist attraction that locals could be proud of led two-thirds of the population to vote in favour of the secession. Not everyone was happy with the idea of King Denys and his 33 fiefs. On news of the declaration of the kingdom, one resident commented – not unreasonably – to the media, 'He's a megalomaniac. He has delusions of grandeur.'

Ladonia

Motto: *Suum Cuique* (To Each His Own)

Founded by a sculptor and constantly at war with neighbouring Sweden for its installations, Ladonia is the micronation for the rebellious artist in everyone. Much like the two founding sculptures – *Arx* and *Nimis* – this nation has stood the test of local councils and bad weather and taken its love of aesthetics to the Swedish government and beyond.

Cyber citizens outweigh residents, but with famous friends such as the artist Christo, Ladonia has always been able to paint itself out of a corner. Plus if things ever get tough they have an ever-expanding cabinet that includes the Ministry of Rock-Paper-Scissors and Ministry of Things Under Rocks.

LOCATION

Ladonia is located on the southern tip of the Scandanavian Peninsula at Kullaberg, surrounded on all sides by Sweden.

FACTS ABOUT LADONIA

WEBSITE www.ladonia.net

FOUNDED 1996

HEAD OF STATE Queen Ywonne I Jarl

HEAD OF GOVERNMENT President Kicki Hankell

LANGUAGE Phrased Latin (official), English, Swedish, Norwegian, Danish, Finnish, German and French (accepted). New citizens are required to choose a Latin phrase and communicate with this phrase only.

CURRENCY Örtug (roughly 10 Swedish crowns)

AREA The nation is a trianglular wedge of roughly 1 sq km

POPULATION Zero (all of its citizens are nomads)

HISTORY

Ladonians trace their history back to when time began, which they believe was when the dragon Ladon had the apples of immortality swiped from him. According to local belief, this introduced a struggle between 'mortal and immortal time', which continues today. There is some historical confusion about King Ladon ruling this particular area of Sweden at some point, but little is known about him other than that he was similarly careless with the golden apples.

Skip a few thousand years to 1980 when sculptor Lars Vilks began crafting two monumental statues: *Nimis* (Latin for 'too much') and *Arx*. Because they were built in an obscure location it was two years before the local council spotted them, despite Nimis being made from 75 tonnes of driftwood. The council immediately ruled that the sculptures were actually houses constructed

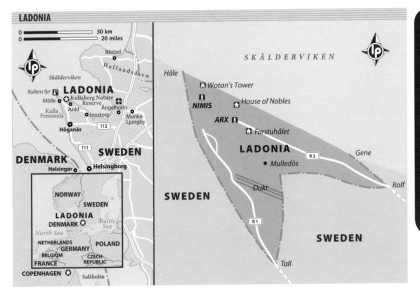

without necessary permits and had to be either removed or destroyed.

Vilks appealed the heavy-handed decision and, after taking it as high as the Swedish national government, was unsuccessful. The problem was partly avoided by the sculptures being bought by the internationally renowned artist Christo, who is famous for wrapping the White Cliffs of Dover in white sheeting. Fearing a similar reprisal on their own landmarks, the Swedish government became reluctant to pursue the matter.

To protect the sculptures, Vilks created the micronation of Ladonia in 1996. In this new nation he cheekily began building another sculpture, *Omphalos*, in 1999. This sculpture was removed, but with council permission Vilks was allowed to erect an 8cm tribute.

FROM A DISTANCE THE MIGHTY *NIMIS* STATUES COULD BE MISTAKEN FOR A VILLAGE – YOU CAN SEE HOW THE COUNCIL GOT IT WRONG

Ladonia was embroiled in further controversy in 2002 when more than 3000 Pakistanis applied to immigrate to the micronation. The nation could not accommodate so many new citizens (all of its existing citizens are nomads, returning only for celebrations) and a clear message on the website was added: 'NB: There is no possibility to receive work or living in Ladonia. Neither visa.'

ECONOMY

Run chiefly by a community of artists, Ladonia was never going to be an economic powerhouse. Tax is not paid in money; instead citizens contribute 'by giving away a part of their creativity'.

The occasional sale of stamps and other merchandise adds to the state coffers, but this is only done when someone has created a design (and the Ministry of Apathy is a powerful force within the government). The creation of nobles is another source of income with regular citizens paying US$12 to have titles the likes of Baron, Lady or Jägermeister.

THINGS TO SEE

ARX

This stone and concrete construction weighs about 150 tonnes with a second almost completed. The sculptor Lars Vilks says it is a 'book with 352 pages which cannot be turned', so the 'reader' of the sculpture must walk around it to 'read'. The highest structure is the 6m-high 'Chapter 2', and the middle section is called 'LUG', named for the Celtic sun god, which includes a gold ring that readers can touch.

NIMIS

Made almost entirely from driftwood, *Nimis* took years to build and is regularly flooded by high tides. The structures are spectacular, with one tower stretching as high as 12m with mirrors to catch the sun. This tower also holds a small statue of Venus.

GETTING THERE & AWAY

Visitors usually enter via Sweden through the border guard at Tall. It's possible to enter the country through other points, but obtaining a visa from the guard at Tall is advised.

CELEBRATING THE ART OF LADONIA DURING A NATIONAL HOLIDAY

Dominion of British West Florida

Regarded (by itself) as a stronghold for British loyalists in North America, the Dominion of West Florida continues to strive for dominion status as a British Commonwealth member (a designation held by countries such as Canada, Australia and New Zealand). This arch-Christian independent nation claims its legitimacy based on the proclamation of 1763, where Britain won the region as spoils from the French and Indian War, exchanging it with the Spanish for Havana, Cuba. The same proclamation established Quebec and Grenada under British rule.

While the region has changed hands several times since the proclamation, subsequent governments are regarded as illegal by the self-proclaimed leadership.

LOCATION

The Dominion of British West Florida lays claim to an area bounded by the Mississippi River and Lake Pontchartrain in the west, by 32.5 degrees latitude to the north, the Gulf of Mexico to the south and the Apalachicola River to the east. For almost 200 years, the area has also been claimed by the US states of Florida, Alabama, Louisiana and Mississippi.

With several million people unknowingly living within the claim, the Dominion of British West Florida has *potentially* the brightest future of any micronation. If the Dominion was ever recognised, it would certainly breathe much-needed new life into the Commonwealth Games and raise the average temperature of British dependencies to something approaching bearable.

FACTS ABOUT BRITISH WEST FLORIDA

WEBSITE www.dbwf.net

FOUNDED 1763 (claim renewed in 2005)

HEAD OF STATE Queen Elizabeth II of England, represented by Acting Governor-General Robert, Duke of Florida

HISTORY

Residents of West Florida – under British rule since 1763 – reacted badly to American Thomas Jefferson's 'petulant letter' (also known as the Declaration of Independence) to King George III in 1776. So the story goes, a mob assembled in a public square, burning effigies of revolutionaries John Adams and John Hancock.

Spain entered the Revolutionary War in 1779, and two years later, in May 1781, had captured West Florida's capital, Pensacola. British loyalists fled. All done? Not on your life! Two years later, in Paris, a treaty was signed ceding control of the region from Britain to Spain. That treaty remains disputed in the Dominion of British West Florida to this day.

US ownership of the region is illegitimate for three reasons: would King George III really have given the proud British loyal-ists of West Florida away to the Catholic Spanish? Theythinks not; that Paris treaty is obviously not valid. And was Spanish authority legitimate anyway, given the installation by Napoleon of a puppet monarchy in Spain? No way, José! And so could the US government have been acting legally when it subsequently annexed the area in 1810? You don't need a doctorate in history to know that the answer is no.

Actually, a doctorate in history would be handy...

RECENT HISTORY

The 'Third Restoration' commenced in November 2005, when the Acting Governor-General Robert, Duke of Florida reasserted Britain's long-held claim on West Florida. Since this time, the Duke has issued a number of proclamations, and has actively sought recognition and diplomatic relations with other macronations and micronations.

CITIZENSHIP

Those lucky enough to be born in the area claimed by West Florida are citizens by birth. 'Loyalists' born anywhere in the British Empire are also granted citizenship if they desire. Others may become citizens by swearing a simple Oath of Allegiance:

I, [Full Name], swear that I will be faithful and bear true allegiance to Her Majesty Queen Elizabeth the Second, by the Grace of God Queen of the UK of Great Britain and Northern Ireland, the Dominion of British West Florida, and Her Other Realms and Territories, Head of the Commonwealth, Defender of the Faith, and Her heirs and successors according to law, and that I will faithfully observe the laws of the Dominion of British West Florida and fulfil my duties as a Dominion of British West Florida citizen.

I, [Full Name], do also swear that I will well and truly serve our Sovereign Lady Queen Elizabeth the Second and will do right to all manner of people, after the laws and usages of the province, without fear or favour, affection or ill-will.

So help me God.

HIS EXCELLENCY, ROBERT, DUKE OF FLORIDA

WEST FLORIDA – BRIT-STYLE

GETTING THERE & AWAY

West Florida is lodged between the states of Louisiana, Mississippi, Alabama, Georgia and Florida. Among the cities found in the Dominion are New Orleans, Baton Rouge, Pensacola, Mobile, Gulfport, Biloxi and Panama City. It is not difficult to reach any of these centres by air, bus or train (Amtrak's Sunset Limited connecting Los Angeles and Orlando is a popular option, serving Pensacola, Mobile and Biloxi three days a week).

LINES OF COMMUNICATION

According to the acting governor-general, the most difficult thing about running West Florida in the name of the British royal family is obtaining clear directions from the palace. The British monarch has not endorsed – or, in all likelihood, even heard of – the claim to West Florida in her name. In correspondence with the author, he wrote:

The most difficult aspect of my duties as Governor-General is to properly determine the Crown's intent. Direct Communication with Her Majesty is hindered by her current ministers, and I'm often left to determine Her intentions based on Tradition and Prior Indications.

All going well, the British monarch will recognise the tireless work of her servant, Robert, and he will receive the recognition, thanks and knighthood he so richly deserves.

Grand Duchy of Elsanor

Motto: Strength Through Solidarity

Describing itself as an enlightened absolute monarchy, the Grand Duchy of Elsanor likens its apparatus of government to that of the Danes in the 19th century. While the grand duchy is a quiet nation, it is currently in a period of expansion, looking for citizens prepared to take an active part in its government.

In January 2006 the ministry of foreign affairs entered into diplomatic relations with two other micronations surrounded by the US: British West Florida (with which it shares neighbouring – possibly overlapping – territorial claims) and the Republic of Molossia. Elsanor also recognises the Principality of Vikesland (landlocked by Canada).

The political leanings of the grand duchy are revealed by its ban on the travel of citizens to China, Iran, Syria and North Korea.

LOCATION

The Grand Duchy of Elsanor is located on a small archipelago (known as the March of Sablon) in the North American Gulf Coast off Alabama and Mississippi. The islands of the archipelago are Pelican Island, Sand Island, and Petit Bois Island, located near the popular vacation spot of Dauphin Island. It also claims land in Northern Alabama (known as the northern provinces).

While sovereignty is currently exercised across the March of Sablon, the government of Elsanor has yet to achieve its goal of ruling the Northern Provinces of Alabama. It proposes to do so in the near future by means of 'political action'.

FACTS ABOUT ELSANOR

WEBSITE www.grandduchyofball.com

FOUNDED Barony of Pelican Island established 1998

HEAD OF STATE His Serene Highness Eric Ball, Grand Duke of Elsanor and Baron of Pelican Island

CAPITAL Pelican Island

NATIONAL DAY 6 January (commemorates the Grand Duke's birthday)

CURRENCY Elsanorian Pound (E); pegged to the US dollar at a rate of one-to-one

TITLE MANIA

The grand duke's full title is His Serene Highness Eric I, of the House of Ball, Most Potent Lord of Elsanor, Earl of Rum, Earl of Traquier, Baron of Pelican Island, Grand Knight Commander of the Noble Order of the Pelican, Grand Knight Commander of the Order of the Rampant Boar, High Knight of the Order of Sablon, Knight of the Order of the Commerant.

IMMIGRATION & DOMESTIC AFFAIRS

Immigration to the grand duchy is possible, with applications assessed on a case-by-case basis. Tourist visas are issued for 15.00E. The ministry of domestic affairs also issues licences to residents for a variety of trades and services, including birth certificates (15.00E), liquor retail licences (5.00E), private prison licences (1000.00E) and oil drilling licences (5.00E).

MILITARY

His Highness' Grand Fleet of Elsanor consists of two 'gunboats', one transport and three lightwater craft. The craft are divided into an East and West Flotilla, protecting the islands of Elsanor.

THINGS TO SEE & DO

PETIT BOIS ISLAND

The largest of the three gulf islands of Elsanor, Petit Bois' 7-sq-km terrain is popular for **camping**, **hiking**, **surfing** and **bird-watching**. This barrier island boasts Mississippi's largest colony of laughing gulls, and is also home to the snowy plover.

SAND ISLAND

Also part of Elsanor's territorial claim, Sand Island is a 3km sand bank just off the east coast of Dauphin Island. Accessible only by boat or jet ski, Sand Island boasts two attractions: the 1884 **Sand Island Lighthouse** and the impressive **point break**, which lures surfers to the eastern side of the island.

DAUPHIN ISLAND

Although this island is located outside of Elsanor's territory, it is nonetheless a noteworthy attraction for visitors to Elsanor. Home to about 1400 people, Dauphin Island draws visitors attracted by the area's natural attractions (particularly **bird-watching** and **fishing**), and the **Fort Gaines Historical Site**.

GETTING THERE & AWAY

Due to competing claims for the Grand Duchy of Elsanor's territory, it is possible for travellers to visit without obtaining specific permission from the government of Elsanor itself. Whether travellers choose to do this, or respect the government and proceed through official channels is up to them.

The islands of the March of Sablon are best reached as a day-trip from popular Dauphin Island, on the western edge of Mobile Bay. Travelling southwest of Mobile on the I-10, Dauphin Island is about 38km along State Hwy 193. The highway ends with a drive across the 6km Dauphin Island Bridge.

From Dauphin Island, Elsanor is just a short boat trip away. Boat hire or charter is available.

HIS SERENE HIGHNESS ON VACATION AT THE ISLE OF CAPRI

MAD AUSSIES

Why do so many Australians decide to start their own country? For some it's about the British queen – either treasuring her as Australia's head of state or ditching her because they've suddenly realised exactly how little the British monarch actually does. Others desire to be liberated from a tyrannical taxation system that asks citizens to pay for trivialities they might not even want, such as schools, roads or art installations. Then there are the guys who just don't want to be flooded...

In a nation of opinionated pub philosophers and talk-back radio addicts, it's surprising that more Australians haven't decided to give their nation the shove. Having a strangely written constitution that gives a European lady authority over Aboriginal people who have a centuries-old ancestral claim on the land seems to just invite people to create their own dominions, principalities and other jumped-up states.

The first Australian micronation could almost have been the state of Western Australia, which during the 1930s was profiting from a local gold rush and was keen to dump the freeloading eastern states, who were going through an economic depression. Western Australians voted to return to being a British colony rather than share their gold booty with the rest of Australia, but Britain rejected the claim then got distracted by WWII and never got back to them. Getting distracted by other global events has proved a good way for many Australians to found their own micronations, including Hutt River (see p22) and Snake Hill Principalities (see p146).

BUMBUNGA & THE STRAWBERRIES

Concerned by Australia's apparent march towards republicanism, ardent monarchist, uranium miner, former monkey trainer and British immigrant, Alex Brackstone, declared his property in South Australia the Province of Bumbunga in 1976, and proclaimed it forever loyal to the British monarchy.

Stamps featuring the British royal family were released, and Governor Brackstone embarked on a plan to raise national funds by creating a tourist attraction on his property. He planted an enormous map of Britain using strawberries. Sadly, the plants died in the harsh Australian sun, and with them, Brackstone's dream of nationhood.

Over the years, Bumbunga appeared in the news a few times, but by the time the governor was brought to trial for firearms charges in 1999, the nation was essentially defunct.

ALEX BRACKSTONE

AVRAM & THE B-WORD

For sheer chutzpah you can't go past the Duchy of Avram. Never formally claiming any territory, the self-proclaimed Duke of Avram, an anti-tax campaigner and kabbala follower, founded the duchy in the early 1980s. In the Tasmanian burg of George Town, he set up the national bank, being his own store, which required customers to swap their Australian dollars for Avram currency to do business. Trying to avoid potential legal problems, the business was called a 'b_nk' and never claimed to be a bank.

The wet-blanket Australian government swept down on Avram, confiscating all currency. Although we haven't been able to confirm it, the Duchy's website claims that the Australian government spent more than A$22 million on six court cases, but was not able to uphold a single charge. The store was closed but the Duke resumed b_nking and last issued coins and banknotes in 2005.

The Duke himself became a local hero, serving as a local member of parliament. He claims the grand title of Cardinal Archbishop of the Royal See and famously has a spot in Who's Who, a paid-for article, possibly using Avram coinage.

RAINBOW CREEK & THE WAR ON VICTORIA

When the Victorian state government built a bridge across the Thompson River in the 1930s, they created a natural disaster. Instead of allowing a safe passage in floods, the bridge was washed over and snagged river debris. Eventually this created a large dam that pushed water across to flood nearby farms. State authorities then had the gall to charge farmers extra fees for water usage (as well as land taxes on their submarine properties).

By the 1970s, the people of this newly created Rainbow Creek had had a gutful and led by retired policeman Thomas Barnes, the farmers declared war on Victoria. With TV cameras rolling, Barnes all but threw the declaration in the face of the Victorian governor. Eventually, the government offered loans to repair properties, but no compensation. Barnes and the farmers weren't interested.

Instead Barnes seceded to form the Independent State of Rainbow Creek, lodging his claims with the still-bemused Victorian governor, Buckingham Palace and the International Court of Justice in the Hague. Passports, stamps and banknotes were all issued to the ire of state officials, but with Barnes ability to find the media spotlight, there was no action against the Rainbow Creek.

Barnes' war was interrupted by poor health and he moved to Queensland in the 1980s, with Rainbow Creek still flowing and presumably remaining an independent state.

UNITED OCEANIA VS UNITED KINGDOM

Another ticked-off ex-copper (low police pensions also factor in Australia's glut of micronations), Peter Gillies had several run-ins with local councils about planning applications on his property near Port Stephens, NSW. The axe fell when Gillies upset authorities with alleged breaches of a worker's contract. Though ruled bankrupt, Prince Peter Gillies declared his 0.66-sq-km land the Principality of United Oceania in 2003. When the Commonwealth of Australia auctioned his property, a citizen of United Oceania bought it on behalf of the principality.

Gillies continued his legal struggle in the UK, arguing that Australia was still a colony and that any decisions made about his property should be made in Britain. Gillies sent emails to most of the Australian senate arguing that Australia had not properly been made independent from Britain and that the only court that had any authority over what he estimated was more than 100 seceded nations in Australia was a British one. In 2005 one UK judge remarked that the case was 'purposeless'.

BIG JOE & LITTLE JOE

In July 2005 the drawbridge was lowered – perhaps for the last time – on the tale of the Principality of Ponderosa. Declared an independent state on 4 July 1994, Ponderosa was a 24 hectare farm near the provincial town of Shepparton, about 150km north of Melbourne.

Virgilio 'Big Joe' Rigoli and his sons Little Joe and Philip angrily declared independence after the department of agriculture bulldozed an infested fruit crop on their property. Surrounding their farm with a moat, the family guarded the boundary, requiring visitors to show passports. Son Philip left the farm in 1997, describing conditions with his family as 'strange and toxic'. Little Joe and his father continued developing their new nation.

In 2001 police raided the breakaway principality, charging the Rigolis with defrauding the Commonwealth of Australia for, among other things, refusing to pay tax. The family ran a polystyrene box business, and refused to pay tax on an estimated income of A\$7 million. At their committal hearing in 2002, the prosecutor quoted poet John Donne's famous statement 'No man is an island, entire of itself'. In their defence, the family claimed they were British subjects, bearing 'alliance' to Queen Elizabeth, and did not recognise Australian governments.

The Ponderosa's constitution decried government policies, including granting land rights to Aborigines and abandoning the law of the Old Testament. An extract from the document describes Ponderosa as a place where 'Christians, white Anglo-Saxons and capitalists are not discriminated against'. Big Joe and Little Joe both received custodial sentences in 2005.

Snake Hill

Motto: *Finis Coronat Opus* (The End Crowns the Work)

If you've ever struggled with accountants, bank loans or lawyers, then Snake Hill is the country for you. Formed after years of wrangling with a difficult mortgage, this family-run nation decided to abandon the Australian legal system after it had abandoned them.

LOCATION

Snake Hill is located 45km from the regional town of Mudgee, northwest of Sydney, Australia.

FACTS ABOUT SNAKE HILL

POSTAL ADDRESS PO Box 488, Baulkham Hills, Australia 2153

WEBSITE www.snakehillprincipality.info

FOUNDED 2003

HEAD OF STATE Prince Paul

LANGUAGE English

AREA The principality is roughly 1.6 sq km in size

EMBASSIES Castle Hill, Sydney; Canada; Philippines; USA

HISTORY

Around the turn of the millennium Prince Paul and Princess Helena were enjoying their two investment properties, but their fairytale was about to end when their lender decided to reclaim their properties. All this was despite the prince actually being ahead on the repayments. When their lender took them to court, Prince Paul, his wife Princess Helena and daughter Princess Paula were shocked that the law supported their lender's right to repossess. It seemed that the lender could foreclose on the loan regardless of how up to date the prince was on his repayments.

After appealing the decision and losing, Prince Paul and his royal family lost faith in the Australian legal system and decided to secede, mainly to draw attention to the injustice and fully expecting to be laughed out of court. But the judge didn't get the joke. As Princess Paula explains it, when a nation's laws don't protect your property you're legally entitled to secede as you've have been 'denied natural justice'.

Since seceding, the principality has corresponded with Australia's prime minister and governor general informing them of the peaceful secession. Princess Paula claims that both have acknowledged the principality as an independent nation (there's no public evidence of this). The principality, however, has assured Queen Elizabeth II that, as a humble principality, they don't question her rule and have also offered her a place to stay if she's ever in Mudgee.

The principality remains unchallenged and maintains all of its property. Today it serves as beacon for others who've had their property taken from them by dubious legal rulings, as well as for victims of property fraud.

ECONOMY

Aside from merchandise (see Shopping, below), the principality has several revenue sources. There are healthy stands of timber, which it intends to export as paper pulp. Plans are underway to build a retirement home in the principality for seniors who are looking for a more competitive tax rate and want to 'retire abroad'. A hotel/palace is also in the pipeline.

GOVERNMENT & POLITICS

The constitution is based on the Ten Commandments and establishes Prince Paul as the ruler of the land, his wife as Princess Helena and his daughter as Crown Princess Paula (in a principality only the ruling prince's wife is a princess). Although a principality, citizens retain the right to vote on all issues.

PEOPLE & CULTURE

At the moment local citizens are limited, but international citizenships are growing.

Lawyers aren't welcomed in Snake Hill. If you've studied law, you might like to explain that you've 'got better' or have received enough counselling to avoid sliding around on your stomach or have overcome your tendency to sneak around behind people with daggers. If you're a lawyer, you should plan to visit another micronation.

Everyone should avoid expressions like 'I rest my case' and 'I'll sue' when visiting Snake Hill.

FACTS FOR THE VISITOR

SHOPPING

The vast majority of Snake Hill's shopping is done online, with a wide variety of T-shirts (US$20), flags (US$10) and passports (US$20) all available. Stamps are also available featuring local wildlife and royal pets.

THINGS TO SEE & DO

SNAKE HILL CHURCH

This simple building hosts Sunday services, which often evolve into counselling sessions where visitors discuss the harshness of their property thefts and share a few lawyer jokes. This has been known to be followed by a delicious Sunday lunch.

PALACE

When completed the palace will be not only a residence for the head of state, but also a hotel with 10 bedrooms.

NATURAL SPRING

This delightful pool is great for swimming and can also make for good fishing when not in drought.

GETTING THERE & AWAY

Mudgee is Snake Hill's closest Australian town, just 45km away. You can get to Mudgee by plane, train, bus or car (just two hours drive northwest of Sydney). Visitors require a visa (US$10) or can purchase a passport (US$20), both available at the border or from the website.

CHURCH INTERIOR – LAWYERS NOT WELCOME

State of Sabotage (SOS)

·············· **Mottoes: A Strategy of Strangers; Solidarity over Sovereignty;** ···············
Subversion of Surveillance

The State of Sabotage has shot out of nowhere to become a player on the micronational scene. SOS originally started out as a virtual 'art' state, heavily influenced by the NSK model (p128), but in 2004 the purchase of 650 hectares of Australian land turned that model into a geographical reality.

SOS has a few defining qualities. For starters, it adheres to the idea that nurturing the arts should be a new state's ultimate aim (rather than sovereignty, commerce or war).

And it has an obsession with the bowels of its citizens.

LOCATION

The capital, Baldrockistan, is 3km from the World Heritage–listed Bald Rock National Park in Queensland, Australia. Stanthorpe is the nearest town, 32km away.

FACTS ABOUT SOS

WEBSITE www.sabotage.at/sos

FOUNDED 2003

HEAD OF STATE Non-President Robert Jelinek

CAPITAL Baldrockistan

LANGUAGES Global

NATIONAL DAY August 30

CURRENCY Cash 50ML

AREA 6.5 sq km

POPULATION 183 citizens; seven residents

HISTORY

SOS sprang from the loins of Sabotage, a small 'art organisation and music label' formed in Vienna, Austria, in 1992.

In 2003 artist Robert Jelinek declared the State of Sabotage in a ritual ceremony on the uninhabited island of Harakka, off the coast of Helsinki, Finland (as part of the Summit of Micronations conference; see p129).

In 2004 SOS purchased land near the **Bald Rock National Park** in Queensland, Australia. The site, dubbed Baldrockistan, was chosen because it's near Tenterfield, where Henry Parkes gave his famous speech advocating the merging of Australian colonies to form a new nation. And centuries ago it was a neutral meeting point for Aboriginal nations: tribal leaders could meet there without having to pass through each other's land. SOS intends to build a hotel, a restaurant and artists' workshops on Baldrockistan, with future programmes to include artist's retreats, residencies and workshops.

In 2005 SOS made headlines when US customs officials confiscated State of Sabotage passports, official stamps and a bottle of Cash perfume from Non-President Robert Jelinek's luggage, reckoning the items would 'in some way be harmful if imported into the US'. It would seem that someone – not naming any names – can't take a joke.

At the time of writing, the SOS had purchased a small plot of land in Lower Austria, with plans to develop this as the second state territory.

GEOGRAPHY & CLIMATE

Baldrockistan is 950m above sea level and the surrounding area is truly spectacular. The national park contains Bald Rock, Australia's largest granite monolith at 1277m, and there are granite domes and towers, canyons, stone arches and an abundance of kangaroos.

Baldrockistan's average year-round temperature is 27°C to 32°C with 70% humidity. In winter temperatures average 10°C to 20°C and 25°C to 38°C in summer.

ECONOMY

As you'd expect from such lovable art rogues, the SOS markets a range of tongue-

NON-PRESIDENT ROBERT JELINEK

SOS' FIRST ATTEMPT TO GAIN TERRITORY MELTED INTO INSIGNIFICANCE

in-cheek 'national' products including Cash perfume, hyped as 'the odour of money – a scent modelled on a freshly printed US$100 bill'. The perfume's slogan is 'CaSH: The Air We Breathe'.

GOVERNMENT

The state's propaganda machine rags out as follows: 'SOS knows neither officials nor functionaries – it knows only self-determined artists and active associates'.

PEOPLE & CULTURE

The people of the State of Sabotage are spiritual and artistic: their immediate plans for Baldrockistan include 'artists' studios and artistic projects emerging in harmony with flora and fauna'.

However, SOS' patron artistic saint is HR Giger, the Swiss master of the macabre, and since when was he ever interested in flowers and cuddly koalas?

FACTS FOR THE VISITOR

PLACES TO STAY & EAT

Bald Rock Retreat (☎ 4686 1227; PO Box 353, Stanthorpe, Qld 4380, Australia; bunks/huts/guestrooms/apt/cabins per person from $30/60/90/125/138) This large nearby Mexican-style hacienda complex runs on solar and wind power. It offers a variety of ranch-style accommodation, home-cooked meals, and beautiful grounds with great views of the national park. Some of the cabins overlook a lake that's good for swimming and fishing.

Memo to the reader: think twice before accepting a dinner invitation from an SOS citizen, for the state's national dish is the maraschino cherry – with a difference. According to official guidelines, the SOS cherry must be prepared with a 'special

THE BALD ROCK MONOLITH

chemical that ensures it will not be digested, but rather will remain lodged in the intestines. It must therefore travel as a lifetime stowaway in the cargo hold of the bowel, like the Flying Dutchman's seabags'.

THINGS TO SEE & DO

Bald Rock, Australia's second largest monolith (1277m above sea level) after Uluru, is a must see – it's in the Bald Rock National Park.

The **Boonoo Boonoo National Park** is 5km north of Baldrockistan. The spectacular Boonoo Boonoo River winds through granite-strewn territory and forest before ending in spectacular 210m-high waterfalls.

GETTING THERE & AWAY

You don't need a visa to enter Baldrockistan, but you will need to show a current SOS passport (these are free and available to anyone, either from their website or in the territory itself).

A NEW LIFE AWAITS YOU IN THE OFFWORLD COLONIES

Some people aspiring to their very own start-up kingdom reckon that the Earth is damned by war and famine and doomed to death and devastation, so their minds turn to outer space and the possibility of vacuum-packed utopias away from Earthly evil.

The earliest, and probably most extreme, example of an extraterrestrial micronation was the **Nation of Celestial Space** (aka Celestia) ruled by James Thompson Mangan. In 1948 Mangan laid claim to outer space in its entirety, going so far as to mint celestial coins and print celestial stamps. Later, he wrote a popular book on salesmanship, although he never managed to sell the idea of Celestia for more than a few years – it folded almost five decades ago.

Back then, the majority of scientists believed we were the only life in the universe, so Mangan's claim that all of space was up for grabs was sound. Now, the tide of opinion says we're not alone, so micronationalists have been looking closer to home – the moon.

As we've seen elsewhere (Sealand, p8; Akhzivland, p48), government territory that is no longer wanted or has been forgotten about is fair game. Sure, the US landed on the moon in 1969, but what right do they really have to our only natural satellite? It's been 36 years now since they first stuck their little flag into that cold, dusty surface and still there's been no development of the land; no settlements – no real indication the US cares about the moon anymore. Do they legally own it after all this time?

Plus they've only claimed a small patch; they haven't even visited most of it.

There's a third argument and it's highly conspiratorial: what if the US never went to the moon? Many people believe that the Apollo missions were faked by the US to save face in a space race they were clearly losing. If true, that would mean the entirety of this lump of rock spinning around the Earth is up for grabs.

In the past, there have been a few micronations that have staked a claim on the moon, but at the time of writing, the lunar kingdoms below were the only two with 'official' Internet details. However, with Virgin Galactic making noises about commercial flights into space in the very near future, this could be an area of micronationalism to keep a close watch on.

THE KINGDOM OF TYCHO

LOCATION Southern Highlands, the moon

WEBSITE www.tycho-kingdom.net

HEAD OF STATE His Royal Highness, King Declan I, Sovereign of The Kingdom of Tycho

CURRENCY TK$ (Tycho Kingdom dollars)

POPULATION Two

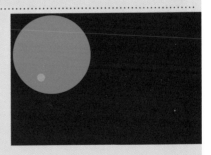

The Kingdom of Tycho appears to be a nation of sci-fi nerds. The culture section of their official website says: 'We need a Culture to be a nation. Si/Fi [sic] and space buffs banding together under a common international (Amercian [sic]/Si/Fi Space exploration) Culture'. They are currently accepting applications for citizenship, but if you really want to be a lunar citizen, you might consider Voodice instead (see p152): they have a 'zero tax' policy, whereas Tycho will slug you one Tycho dollar for every 2 sq km of Tychonian land you own. The Tycho website also includes this ominous warning: 'You may be committing a crime by being a citizen of the Kingdom of Tycho. You may face persecution. With this in mind you should think carefully before you apply for citizenship of the Kingdom of Tycho.' Couldn't have said it better ourselves.

THE PRINCIPALITY OF VOODICE

HEAD OF STATE Prince Karel I

CURRENCY US dollars

AREA 25 sq km

POPULATION 52

LOCATION Area L–7 Quadrant Charlie, the moon

WEBSITE www.voodice.info

Not much is known about the Principality of Voodice, except that it refuses to tax its citizens and claims to have diplomatic representations with the Czech Republic and Slovakia.

FURTHER READING

- **Artemis Project** (www.asi.org) The extensive website of 'a private venture to establish a permanent, self-supporting community on the Moon'.
- **The Men Who Sold the Moon** (2006) by Virgiliu Pop. Charts the history of various claimants to the moon and beyond, with a chapter on the Nation of Celestial Space.

The Authors

JOHN RYAN

John Ryan was the co-ordinating author of this book and was responsible for its conception. He wrote everything except as attributed below.

John has had hundreds of articles published in major (and minor) Australian newspapers and magazines over the past decade. His career highlight was being quoted briefly in the *New Yorker* magazine in 2005. John clicked through 823 results of a Google search for his name, didn't find himself, and decided to write a book. This is his first book, and – based on the lightweight ideas floating around in his head – could well be his last. For Lonely Planet, John has written small pieces on Australian football and having relationships while travelling. John knows very little about either of these things. John calls Melbourne home and Lonely Planet work.

GEORGE DUNFORD

George Dunford wrote the profiles for Christiania, Whangamomona, North Dumpling, Saugeais, Barony of Caux, Ladonia, and Snake Hill and the boxed text From the Sea, Freedom (with John Ryan) and Mad Aussies (with John Ryan).

Getting lost on the Forgotten World Hwy while researching Lonely Planet's New Zealand took George Dunford to the unremembered nation of Whangamomona. He was so impressed by their independence, local brew and experimental jewellery that he wanted to know more. When he's not testing the unstackability of Christiania bikes or Googling Dean Kamen in a way that verges on stalking, he's a freelance writer working out of the People's Republic of Flemington (unrecognised by all but its mother). During the research and writing of this book he may have had a beard or just missed a spot while shaving.

SIMON SELLARS

Simon Sellars wrote the Kugelmugel, Akhzivland, Copeman Empire, State of Sabotage, Gay and Lesbian Kingdom, Romkerhall and Elleore profiles. He also wrote the Redonda, Cascadia, Offworld Colonies and Cybernerds boxed texts.

Simon is a freelance writer and editor. He's been fascinated by micronations ever since he formed the Independent Republic of Bentleigh at the age of 16. Declaring himself president, Simon seceded the IRB from Australia, claiming the Melbourne suburb of Bentleigh as IRB territory and the Rose Tattoo song 'We Can't Be Beaten' as the national anthem. Unfortunately the republic was invaded by Poland and forced to disband in late '83 when Miroslav Murawski, the Polish kid from next door, jumped the fence and beat Simon up for his lunch money, thereby bleeding the entirety of the IRB's national assets (and the president's nose) in one savage blow.

CONTRIBUTING AUTHOR

Simon Hall wrote the section on Cinderella Stamps. Simon is a writer who works in a stamp shop in his spare time.

Thanks

FROM JOHN

Thank you to the micronational leaders and lackeys who provided information and support for this book, especially President Baugh of Molossia, Jessica Pachler from the Maritime Republic of Eastport and R Ben Madison, founder of Talossa.

Thanks also to those people, nations and organisations that provided images. Special call-outs to Kim Gilmour, Lachlan Ross, Prince Leonard and George II, Emperor of Atlantium.

Thanks to the crew at Lonely Planet, especially Bridget Blair, Chris Rennie, Roz Hopkins and the sales and marketing teams, and to my fellow writers George and Simon. Thanks also to the blokes at the Mountain Goat Brewery – I've never met you, but I think your Hightail Ale is tops.

This book is for Elissa and Seamus, queen and prince of the little nation we've made in Brunswick.

FROM GEORGE

First nod belongs to the mighty monarch Good King John Ryan for conceiving and delivering this little baby, all while adding to the Ryan clan. Thanks also to Baroness Bridget Blair for bringing me on board (and tolerating some strained alliteration) and to co-author Simon Sellars for keeping it saucy. And a wink that could be a facial twitch to travel companion to the stars and Earl of Whirl, Simon Hall. A tousle of the hair to Tommy Boy Kelly for shedding light on NZ's second-largest nation. Nuggets of gratitude to Nikki Anderson for the translations and tribulations ('Who are these freaks?').

I'd also like to shout Murt and Margaret Kennard a whopping Whanga burger for the presidential audience. Thanks to the micronationalists who answered my many annoying questions: Princess Paula, Lord John Corbett of Caux, Leif 'Asterix' Botwell and Lars Vilks. Big cheers to Peter Santos (www.psbikes.com.au) for the spin on a genuine Christiania bike.

Thanks also to the photographic contributions of Bob Muller (author of *Long Island's Lighthouses: Past and Present* and www.longislandlighthouses.com) and Christian Voulgaropoulos.

FROM SIMON

Thanks to John Ryan for initiating this project and inviting me to work on it, and to Justine Vaisutis for invaluable support behind the scenes. Thanks also to Bridget Blair at Lonely Planet and co-author George Dunford, and also to Nana Marckmann, Oliver Croy, Sandra Mack and Rachel Thorpe for translations.

Finally, many, many thanks to all the micronationalists and all the kings and queens in this book for your inspiration and courage in following your vision. May you never suffer the fate of the IRB.

CREDITS

This book was produced in Lonely Planet's Melbourne office. It was commissioned by Bridget Blair and overseen by publishing manager Chris Rennie. Jenny Bilos managed the project with assistance from Annelies Mertens and production manager Jo Vraca. Simon Williamson edited with assistance from Martine Lleonart and Branislava Vladisavljevic. The book was designed by James Hardy and laid out by Michael Ruff, and Mark Adams designed the cover. Wayne Murphy created the maps, and Michael Ruff managed pre-press preparation of the photographs.

ACKNOWLEDGEMENTS

Lonely Planet gratefully acknowledges the participation and kind assistance of the micronations in this book.

The images on the following pages were supplied by Lonely Planet Images: 14, 15, 130, 132, 134, 141.

Index

MAP LEGEND

ROUTES

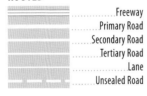

......................Freeway
.....................Primary Road
....................Secondary Road
..................Tertiary Road
.............................Lane
.................Unsealed Road

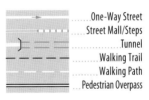

...................One-Way Street
..................Street Mall/Steps
..........................Tunnel
......................Walking Trail
......................Walking Path
...............Pedestrian Overpass

TRANSPORT

....................Ferry
....................Metro
....................Airfield
.........Border Crossing

.....................Rail
.....................Metro
.....................Airport
.................Heliport

HYDROGRAPHY

..................River, Creek
.........Swamp, Everglades
.......................Reef

..................Ocean, Lakes
.........Glacier/Ice Shelf

BOUNDARIES

.............International
.........State, Provincial

..........Regional, Suburb
.............Marine Border

AREA FEATURES

..............Area of Interest
..............Beach, Desert
...................Building
...................Campus
......Cemetery, Christian

.....Forest, National Park
.......................Land
.......................Park
.................Reservation
.....................Urban

POPULATION

CAPITAL (MICRONATION)
Large City
Small City

CAPITAL (NATION)
Medium City
Town, Village

SYMBOLS

........................Beach
...........................Café
...........................Flag
...........................Fort
.....................Grill, BBQ
............House, Building
..................Lighthouse
...........................Mine
........Mountain, Volcano

.... Museum, Gallery
.... National Park
.... Pass, Canyon
.... Point of Interest
.... Rådhus
.... Ruin
.... Sculpture
.... Shelter, Hut
.... Winter Sports

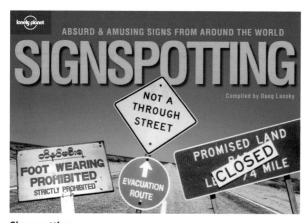

Signspotting

By Doug Lanksy

Anyone who has spent time on the road knows that you often have to depend on signs...to navigate through a town, locate your hotel, even obey the law. A scary thought if you've ever come across any of the publicly posted absurdities that appear in this book. Signs about as easy to understand as a Swahili auctioneer (to a non-Swahili speaker) or as well-planned as the dance steps in a mosh pit. With the help of signspotters around the globe, we've assembled a collection of some of of the most unintentionally entertaining postings on the planet.

By the Seat of My Pants

Edited by Don George

Lonely Planet knows that some of life's funniest experiences happen on the road. Whether they take the form of unexpected detours, unintended adventures, unidentifiable dinners or unforgettable encounters, these experiences can give birth to our most profound travel lessons and illuminations, and our most memorable – and hilarious – travel stories. This collection presents 31 globe-girdling tales that run the gamut from close-encounter safaris to loss-of-face follies, hair-raising rides to culture-leaping brides, eccentric expats to mind-boggling repasts, wrong roads taken to agreements mistaken. The collection brings together some of the world's most renowned travellers and storytellers with previously unpublished writers.

"Sick of sightseeing?
Tired of tour guides?
Then why not try
Experimental Tourism,
a novel approach to travel
that starts with a quirky
concept and can lead
anywhere from Bora Bora
to a bus stop".
CNN.com

The Lonely Planet Guide to
EXPERIMENTAL
TRAVEL

The Lonely Planet Guide to Experimental Travel

By Rachael Antony and Joel Henry

The new phenomenon of experimental tourism, developed by Joel Henry, founder of the Laboratory of Experimental Tourism, has turned the traditional way we travel on its head. This humorous, engaging and practical guide taps into the current interest in exploring different ways of seeing and behaving. Part philosophy, part travel guide and at times surreal, this user-friendly, tongue-in-cheek manual-style book includes practical experiments to follow both while travelling and when at home.

THIS IS NOT
THE END

www.lonelyplanet.com